Reclaiming Unlived 1

In *Reclaiming Unlived Life*, influential psychoanalyst Thomas H. Ogden uses rich clinical examples to illustrate how different types of thinking may promote or impede analytic work. With a unique style of "creative reading," the book builds upon the work of Winnicott and Bion, discussing the universality of unlived life and the ways unlived life may be reclaimed in the analytic experience. The book examines the role of intuition in analytic practice and the process of developing an analytic style that is uniquely one's own.

Ogden deals with many forms of interplay of truth and psychic change, the transformative effect of conscious and unconscious efforts to confront the truth of experience, and how psychoanalysts can understand their own psychic evolution, as well as that of their patients. *Reclaiming Unlived Life* sets out a new way that analysts can understand and use notions of truth in their clinical work and in their reading of the work of Kafka and Borges.

Reclaiming Unlived Life: Experiences in Psychoanalysis will appeal to psychoanalysts and psychoanalytic psychotherapists, as well as postgraduate students and anybody interested in the literature of psychoanalysis.

Thomas H. Ogden, MD, has published eleven books of essays on the theory and practice of psychoanalysis, most recently *Creative Readings: Essays on Seminal Analytic Works*; *Rediscovering Psychoanalysis*; and *This Art of Psychoanalysis*. His work has been translated into more than twenty languages. He was awarded the 2012 Sigourney Award for his contributions to the field of psychoanalysis. He has also published two novels: *The Parts Left Out* and *The Hands of Gravity and Chance*.

THE NEW LIBRARY OF PSYCHOANALYSIS
General Editor: Alessandra Lemma

The New Library of Psychoanalysis was launched in 1987 in association with the Institute of Psychoanalysis, London. It took over from the International Psychoanalytical Library which published many of the early translations of the works of Freud and the writings of most of the leading British and Continental psychoanalysts.

The purpose of the New Library of Psychoanalysis is to facilitate a greater and more widespread appreciation of psychoanalysis and to provide a forum for increasing mutual understanding between psychoanalysts and those working in other disciplines such as the social sciences, medicine, philosophy, history, linguistics, literature and the arts. It aims to represent different trends both in British psychoanalysis and in psychoanalysis generally. The New Library of Psychoanalysis is well placed to make available to the English-speaking world psychoanalytic writings from other European countries and to increase the interchange of ideas between British and American psychoanalysts.

The Institute, together with the British Psychoanalytical Society, runs a low-fee psychoanalytic clinic, organizes lectures and scientific events concerned with psycho-analysis and publishes the International Journal of Psychoanalysis. It runs a training course in psychoanalysis which leads to membership of the International Psychoanalytical Association – the body which preserves internationally agreed standards of training, of professional entry, and of professional ethics and practice for psychoanalysis as initiated and developed by Sigmund Freud.

Distinguished members of the Institute have included Michael Balint, Wilfred Bion, Ronald Fairbairn, Anna Freud, Ernest Jones, Melanie Klein, John Rickman and Donald Winnicott. Current members of the Advisory Board include Giovanna Di Ceglie, Liz Allison, Anne Patterson, Josh Cohen and Daniel Pick.

For a full list of all the titles in the New Library of Psychoanalysis main series as well as both the New Library of Psychoanalysis Teaching and 'Beyond the Couch' subseries, please visit the Routledge website.

RECENT TITLES IN THIS SERIES:

THE NEW LIBRARY OF PSYCHOANALYSIS

General Editor: Alessandra Lemma

Reclaiming Unlived Life

Experiences in Psychoanalysis

Thomas H. Ogden

Routledge
Taylor & Francis Group

LONDON AND NEW YORK

First published 2016
by Routledge
2 Park Square, Milton Park, Abingdon, Oxon OX14 4RN

and by Routledge
711 Third Avenue, New York, NY 10017

Routledge is an imprint of the Taylor & Francis Group, an informa business

© 2016 Thomas H. Ogden

British Library Cataloguing in Publication Data
A catalogue record for this book is available from the British Library

Library of Congress Cataloging in Publication Data
Names: Ogden, Thomas H.
Title: Reclaiming unlived life : experiences in psychoanalysis / Thomas H.
Ogden.
Description: Abingdon, Oxon ; New York, NY : Routledge, 2016. | Includes
bibliographical references and index.
Identifiers: LCCN 2015046984| ISBN 9781138955998 (hardback) | ISBN
9781138956018 (pbk.)
Subjects: LCSH: Psychoanalysis.
Classification: LCC RC506 .O3427 2016 | DDC 616.89/17—dc23
LC record available at http://lccn.loc.gov/2015046984

ISBN: 978-1-138-95599-8 (hbk)
ISBN: 978-1-138-95601-8 (pbk)
ISBN: 978-1-315-66594-8 (ebk)

Typeset in Bembo
by Florence Production Ltd, Stoodleigh, Devon, UK

For SPO

Contents

Acknowledgments

I would like to thank *The Psychoanalytic Quarterly* for permission to use the following papers in this volume:

Kafka, Borges, and the creation of consciousness. Part I. Kafka: Dark ironies of the "gift" of consciousness. *Psychoanalytic Quarterly* 78: 343–367, 2009. Copyright *The Psychoanalytic Quarterly*.

Kafka, Borges, and the creation of consciousness. Part II. Borges: A life of letters encompassing everything and nothing. *Psychoanalytic Quarterly* 78: 369–396, 2009. Copyright *The Psychoanalytic Quarterly*.

On three types of thinking: magical thinking, dream thinking, and transformative thinking. *Psychoanalytic Quarterly* 79: 314–347, 2010. Copyright *The Psychoanalytic Quarterly*.

Intuiting the truth of what's happening: On Bion's "Notes on memory and desire." *Psychoanalytic Quarterly* 84: 285–306, 2015. Copyright *The Psychoanalytic Quarterly*.

The *International Journal of Psychoanalysis* has kindly granted permission to use the following papers in this volume:

Fear of breakdown and the unlived life. *International Journal of Psychoanalysis* 91: 205–224, 2014. Copyright The Institute of Psychoanalysis.

On becoming a psychoanalyst (co-authored with G. O. Gabbard). *International Journal of Psychoanalysis* 90: 311–327, 2009. Copyright The Institute of Psychoanalysis.

I am grateful to *Rivista di Psicoanalisi* (The Journal of the Italian Psychoanalytic Society) for permission to publish:

Thomas H. Ogden in conversation with Luca Di Donna. *Rivista di Psicoanalisi* 59: 625–641, 2013. Copyright *Rivista di Psicoanalisi*.

I would like to thank Dr. Glen Gabbard for the creative collaboration that went into our co-authored paper "On becoming a psychoanalyst" (Chapter 5 of this volume) and Dr. Luca di Donna for the intelligence and imagination he brought to the conversation that comprises the final chapter of this book. I am grateful to Dr. Marta Schneider Brody for her insightful editorial comments on several chapters of this book, and to Gina Atkinson and Patricia Marra for the thought and care they put into preparing this book for publication.

TRUTH AND PSYCHIC CHANGE

In place of an introduction

Periodically, I try to find out who I have become, and am becoming, as a psychoanalyst by writing about that process as best I can (see Ogden, 1994, 1997a, 1997b, 2004, 2009). It is difficult to know where to start in this endeavor, but a point of departure that feels right to me now is that I must invent psychoanalysis freshly with each patient. In what follows, I address different aspects of the way I work as an analyst, while knowing at the outset that these parts cannot possibly come together as an integrated whole that accurately reflects my experience. But, by the act of laying them out here for myself and the reader, I hope they may be of use to the reader in gaining an understanding of how he or she practices psychoanalysis and may provide the beginnings of lines of thought with which the reader may make something of his or her own.

I find myself talking with each patient in a different way, with different tones of voice, different ranges of pitch, volume, and cadences of speech, different syntax and word choice, and in doing so communicate what cannot be said in any other way to any other person. This is not surprising to me in that I do not talk with one of my two grown children in the way I talk to the other; I did not talk with my father, at any stage of my life, as I did with my mother; I do not talk to my wife in a way that I do with anyone else. Each person with whom I enter into intimate conversation draws on me, and I draw on him or her, in such a way that I become a different person to some degree, and speak differently with each of these people. The more intimate the conversation, the more this is true.

The conversations I have with my patients are among the most intimate that I have in my life.

I believe that each of my patients would be surprised to overhear the way I talk with any other patient. The way I talk with one patient would feel foreign to any other; what I say to one patient, and the way I say it, would sound too fraternal, too maternal, too formal, too something to another patient. To put it another way, one of my patients would, I believe, feel that the way I talk to any other patient does not suit her, and she would be right, because it was not meant for her, it was not created *with* her and *for* her.

The rhythm of the verbal exchange in my analytic work is also unique to each patient. The rhythm is not that of extended periods of silence while the patient talks, punctuated now and again by a comment on my part. Neither is it the rhythm of ordinary conversation outside the consulting room. The rhythm of the analytic conversation is unlike the rhythm of any other type of conversation. There are several interrelated reasons for this.

First, the setting in which the analytic conversation takes place is designed to provide the patient and analyst the opportunity for dreaming in such forms as waking dreaming (reverie), "talking-as-dreaming" (Ogden, 2007), "dream thinking," and "transformative thinking" (see Chapter 2 for discussions of dream thinking and transformative thinking). In an effort to create a space for dreaming (other than in the initial consultation session or sessions), I sit behind the couch while the patient lies on the couch. I explain to each of my patients at the outset of an analysis that their use of the couch allows me the privacy I need to think in a way that differs from the way I think in face-to-face conversation. I add that the patient may find that this is true for him or her, too. I work with patients on the couch regardless of the frequency of our sessions.

Second, I do not adhere to Freud's (1912) "fundamental rule." I have found both in my own experience and in the work of analysts who consult with me that the injunction to "say everything that comes to mind" compromises the patient's right to privacy, which is necessary for the freedom to dream in the session. So, rather than asking the patient to say everything that comes to mind, I tell the patient (sometimes explicitly, sometimes implicitly) that she is free to say whatever she wants to say and to keep to herself what she chooses—and that I will do the same (Ogden, 1996).

The upshot of these aspects of containment in the session (management of the analytic frame) is a rhythm of conversation that differs from any other conversation. It is a rhythm in which I am always present (always listening, sometimes talking) as the patient and I move in and out of various forms of dreaming. Waking up from dreaming in the analytic session is as important as the inherent therapeutic value of dreaming itself. Put another way, talking *about* dreaming—understanding something about the meaning of our dreaming—is, to my mind, an essential part of the therapeutic process.

The combination of these and other features of the analytic endeavor—including the fact that it is primarily designed to serve the function of helping the patient achieve psychological growth—contribute to the unique rhythms of the analytic conversation. That rhythm differs with each patient, and within each hour, but by and large involves an active interchange in which the patient speaks more than I do, yet neither of us "dominates" the conversation. I do not limit myself to brief statements. Now and again, I find myself talking at considerable length, at times telling the patient a story (sometimes a story the patient already knows, but pretends not to know so he or she can hear me tell it to them). As is the case with virtually everything else in the analytic relationship, the flow of conversation is a creation that only *this* patient and *this* analyst (the analyst I am becoming in the analysis) could bring to life in *this* particular way.

When I am not creating psychoanalysis *with* and *for* a given patient, the analysis feels generic and impersonal, both to the patient and to me. I am often bored during such sessions and may even fall asleep. Falling asleep under those circumstances is a signal to me that I am not able to dream the session *with* the patient, and may be unconsciously evading that work by attempting to "dream the session" on my own.

I conceive of my work as a psychoanalyst as that of dreaming *with* the patient aspects of his experience that have been too painful for him to dream on his own (Ogden, 2004). I use the term *dreaming* to refer to unconscious thinking, which I believe to be the richest form of thinking that human beings are capable of because it simultaneously brings to bear on an emotional problem a multiplicity of types of thinking—primary and secondary process thinking, synchronic and diachronic senses of time, cause-and-effect thinking, and thinking that releases the two from a sequential relationship (see Chapter 2 for further elaboration of this conception of "dreamthinking").

It is impossible to say "where an idea comes from." My principal psychoanalytic teachers have been Freud, Klein, Fairbairn, Winnicott, Bion, Loewald, and Searles, but I have learned as much about

3

psychoanalysis from poets, novelists, and playwrights. From one perspective, every sentence that I write about "my" way of practicing psychoanalysis ought to have a string of references appended to it in order to give credit to the people who have contributed to the development of the ideas I am discussing. And yet, from another perspective, no references at all are called for because what I make with their work is uniquely my own.

In the course of my life, I have been fundamentally altered by my experiences with my parents and with the three analysts with whom I have worked. I am fortunate to be able to say that the ways I have been changed by these experiences have been predominantly enriching and growth promoting. Nonetheless, I have come to feel that I have a responsibility to become a better analyst than they were able to be for me. I feel the same responsibility holds true of the succession of generations of parents and their children. Fulfilling the responsibility to do better than they (both one's analyst and one's parents) is not an act of protest or revolt; it is an effort to make full use of them. I know that my parents wished that they could have been better parents to me, and I imagine my analysts felt something similar. This felt desire on the part of my parents was terribly important in my developing a need to imagine ("dream up") a way of becoming a better parent to my children and a better analyst to my patients. When I am with my grandchildren, it is clear to me that my son is a better father than I was to him. This does not cause me to feel rejected or vanquished by him; quite the contrary, what greater gift could a child give a parent?

When I speak of a child or patient becoming a "better parent" or a "better analyst" than his or her parents or analyst, I have in mind (along with a great many other qualities) the child's (or analysand's) developing an enhanced capacity to carry the pain of the child or patient until the child or analysand has sufficiently matured to be able to carry it for himself or herself. In the succession of generations, of equal importance to the parent's or analyst's ability to carry the pain of the child or patient is their capacity, at each step of development, to return to the child or patient *his own* pain, because it is *his* (the child's or patient's) and is a vital part of his sense of self. This holds true even, or perhaps more accurately, *particularly*, for a person's traumatic experience. The individual is killed off to the degree that the experience of trauma is left "unlived." The parent's and analyst's act of returning to the child or patient the responsibility for his pain is as difficult as carrying it, for to return it is to surrender a source of the parent's or analyst's sense of being needed, a feeling that is incomparably gratifying and self-affirming, and incredibly difficult to give up.

I find that psychoanalytic theory is not a thing apart from my experience with patients in the consulting room. While working with patients, analytic ideas are always in the wings. Even when analytic theory is out of my conscious thoughts, it nonetheless constitutes a "matrix" (a psychic context, a metaphorical womb) that sculpts the way I hold an experience while working with a patient. How could such fundamental ideas as the unconscious (in an analytic sense that few people other than analysts genuinely comprehend), dreaming (again, in the sense that only analysts understand), reverie, transference, infantile and childhood sexuality, and fear of breakdown not be part of the very structure of my mind and of my thinking at this point in my life? Theory becomes an encumbrance to me only when I find that I am using it in a way that answers, as opposed to frames or poses, questions.

The role of analytic theory varies greatly from patient to patient, and also from hour to hour, and minute to minute with any given patient. There are innumerable circumstances in which theory has played an important role in my analytic work. For reasons I cannot explain, an instance that comes to mind is one in which my thinking about analytic theory while with a patient served as a necessary way of distancing myself from what was happening in the session. I felt in the course of years of analytic work with Mr. A that I was living *his* psychotic terrors of disappearing into empty space, and that I was absolutely alone with them. This was something I could not bear indefinitely. I found myself puzzling in the sessions over matters of analytic theory, realizing only later that I was doing so in a way that felt like a conversation with (sane) people who were interested in, and knowledgeable about, analytic theories of primitive mental states. Engaging with theory (and imaginary theorists) in this way helped me tolerate what the patient was evoking in me long enough to see that period of work through.

I have now, many years after my work with Mr. A has come to an end, come to view this engagement with theory of primitive terror (and the theorists who have developed it) as a reverie experience in which I was discovering that it was not necessary to live the primitive terrors indefinitely *on my own*. I strongly believe that that realization, though I did not speak with Mr. A about it, was an essential communication to him that he, too, need not live indefinitely his terrors *by himself*. In this instance, analytic theory was not simply a set of ideas, it was a sane (meaning-generating and symbol-generating) language in which I could talk with myself during sessions, between sessions, and long after the sessions had occurred. (Of course, this is not a paradigm for the role of theory in clinical practice; rather, it is an example of a single experience.)

The idea that the human mind needs the truth as much as we need food and water (Bion, 1962a, p. 32), and that our minds—the unconscious aspect of our minds, in particular—are continuously in search of the truth, has become central to my current conception of the analytic process. Being in touch with (intuiting) the truth of what is occurring at any moment in an analytic session, to my mind, is closely connected with the phenomenon of aliveness of the session. When a session does not feel alive, it feels to me, and to the patient as well, that we are not engaged in an experience that feels truthful. It is not that we are "lying" or "resisting" (terms that feel moralistic, and consequently destructive to an effort to think); rather, we are fearful of the truth of what is occurring at that moment (Ogden, 1995).

The repercussions of the idea that the unconscious has not only a meaning-making function, but a truth-seeking function (Grotstein, 2007; see also Chapter 4), are multifold in my clinical work. As I write this, I am reminded of an experience that occurred in my work with Mr. C, a patient with cerebral palsy. My omnipotent wishes to "cure" him of his cerebral palsy served to protect me from facing a truth: I was unable to accept the patient as he was, just as his mother had been unable to manage the fact that her son was born with a serious handicap. She raged at him, calling him a monster. I did not rage at him, but I was unable to accept him for who he was. It took me a long time to see that in unconscious fantasy I experienced him as a defective version of the person he would have been (and worse yet, should have been), were he not a person impaired by cerebral palsy. The development of my capacity to live with the truth of his cerebral palsy was manifested, as the therapy progressed, in the form of my love (no other word suffices) for this patient just as he was.

Late in our work together, Mr. C told me a dream: "Not much happened in the dream. I was myself with my cerebral palsy, washing my car and enjoying listening to music on the car radio that I had turned up loud." This was the first time that Mr. C specifically mentioned his cerebral palsy while telling me a dream. Moreover, the language he used to say it—"I was myself with my cerebral palsy"—was striking. How better could he have expressed a depth of recognition and acceptance of himself? In the dream, he was able to be a mother who took pleasure in bathing her baby (his car) while listening to and enjoying the music that was coming from inside the baby. This was not a dream of triumph; it was an ordinary dream of ordinary love: "nothing much happened."

I was deeply moved by the patient's telling me his dream. I said to him, "What a wonderful dream that was." In saying this, I was both living the experience of the dream with Mr. C, and speaking as a separate person observing the truth of who he was in the process of becoming (in the dream, in relation to me, and in the world outside of the consulting room).

Only after I had done the psychological work of accepting this patient as he was, could he, for the first time in his life, experience a form of being loved, and accepting himself for who he was, that felt real (true, alive), even as he bellowed in pain, and tears and saliva and nasal mucus ran down his large, palsied face. I felt toward him as I later felt toward my two children when they were infants in the grip of wordless, shapeless fear and pain. My experience with this patient helped me grow up as an analyst and as a (future) father and grandfather. Mr. C remains very much alive in me almost forty years after our work together ended. (See Ogden, 2010, for further discussion of the analysis of Mr. C.)

The idea that human beings have a powerful need for truth has further implications for me. The need for the truth is not a policing function (keeping oneself honest); it is more an expression of a need for the "freedom to think" the reality of one's experience (Symington, 1983), which is essential to psychoanalysis as a therapeutic process. My role as an analyst is to help the patient mature in ways that allow him to better encompass the realities of his emotional life. Helping a patient face the truth of his experience need not be a confrontational experience. I do not point out the truth to the patient, I live it with the patient until he or she is able to experience it on his own and express it in verbal or nonverbal ways. Integral to facing the truth is the patient's trust in me, and my trustworthiness. "The sacred space of fully open listening, reading, and conversing requires the vulnerability of maximal trust, trust in the essential benevolence of the other, and trust in the resilience of one's self to be able to come apart and even be changed significantly without losing one's essential sense of self" (Warren Poland, personal communication, 2014).

I find most valuable those analytic theories that attempt to provide fresh metaphors for the truths of human emotional experience.

Theory of this sort tends to abjure analytic nomenclature and instead attempts to describe what happened from a vantage point that feels original and true to me. In other words, language is not just a basket in which ideas are carried: the way in which language is used to state an idea is inseparable from the content of the idea.

I cannot resist illustrating the idea of the inseparability of style and content by citing a passage from Winnicott's "Primitive emotional development" (1945, p. 152), a paper I treasure both for the brilliance of the writing and the brilliance of the thinking:

> . . . the baby has instinctual urges and predatory ideas. The mother has a breast and the power to produce milk, and the idea that she would like to be attacked by a hungry baby. These two phenomena do not come into relation with each other till the mother and child *live an experience together*. The mother being mature and physically able has to be the one with tolerance and understanding, so that it is she that produces a situation which may with luck result in the first tie the infant makes with an external object, that is external to self from the infant's point of view.

Winnicott here tells a story of a "predatory baby" (a villain in diapers) who "attacks" the mother; and the story of his mother who, with her breasts full of milk, "would like to be attacked" by this villain (whose vitality and gusto she adores, though being attacked again and again can be taxing). This convergence of passions (*desire* would be too weak a word) allows the two to "*live an experience together*" (such a simple way of stating an idea that has altered the course of the development of analytic thinking). The paradox of simultaneous separateness (the attack of the baby on the mother, and the mother's welcoming the attack) and oneness (the infant and mother *living an experience together*) is the experiential medium for "the first tie the infant makes with an external object, that is external to self from the infant's point of view."

In his understated way, Winnicott introduces here a radically new conception of the birth of the infant's recognition of his mother as external to himself, and in so doing comes to recognize himself as separate from her. Only by inference does Winnicott also introduce the idea that the infant's attaining the ability to have a "point of view" (as a person separate not only from his mother, but also from himself) represents the birth of human consciousness (self-awareness).

The "stories" that Winnicott tells in this handful of sentences cannot be told in any other words without significant loss of meaning.

There are many other examples of the inseparability of style and content in analytic theory. A few that I find not only cogent, but beautiful, immediately come to mind:

Freud: "In mourning it is the world which has become poor and empty; in melancholia it is the ego itself" (1917, p. 246).

Loewald: "If we do not shrink from blunt language, in our role as children of our parents, by genuine emancipation we do kill something vital in them—not all in one blow and not in all respects, but contributing to their dying" (1979, p. 395).

Bion: "The patient who cannot dream cannot go to sleep and cannot wake up. Hence the peculiar condition seen clinically when the psychotic patient behaves as if he were in precisely this state" (1962a, p. 7).

The acts of "explaining" and "understanding" have always felt like very different categories of experience, but recently the differences between the two have served to highlight principles of practice that are particularly important to me. A stereotypic example of explaining something to a patient might sound like this: "I think that you overslept this morning and missed most of the session because your expression of gratitude to me as you left our session yesterday frightened you." A principal shortcoming, to my mind, in this interpretation, even if it were in some sense accurate, is that it objectifies the patient. The analyst is talking *about* the patient, not *with* the patient. The explanation relies heavily on conscious, secondary process thinking even as it purports to address the workings of the patient's unconscious. Human response to experience does not obey the laws of cause-and-effect logic or of sequential time. We are the totality of our life's experience as we live the present moment. The past is not "behind us," it is in us. The unconscious is not "timeless," it is full of time (the entirety of our lives).

In contrast with explaining, *understanding* in the analytic setting begins with the experience of patient and analyst "*liv*[ing] *an experience together*" (Winnicott, 1945, p. 152) that Winnicott introduced in the passage I quoted earlier. This *phase of the development of understanding* entails a relatively primitive, somewhat undifferentiated form of communication of feeling between patient and analyst, and between

9

mother and infant. By drawing on this early form of communication, the experience of understanding comes to involve a paradox: understanding is a far more intimate form of communication than explanation, while at the same time it necessarily includes, as it evolves, the patient's and the analyst's awareness of their separateness. In other words, "understanding" in the analytic setting, as I view it and as I experience it, involves the recognition on the part of both patient and analyst that they are two separate people with two separate minds: I am other to you, and you are other to me. Thus, the experience of the analyst's understanding of the patient paradoxically involves simultaneous *at-one-ment* and separateness. If there were no divide of this sort underlying my understanding of the patient—that I am an "other"—the patient might as well be talking to himself.

"Understanding," in this sense, is an ontological phenomenon, an experience in which an aspect of one's essential being is recognized by another person. This can be achieved only in a relationship in which there is, for both patient and analyst, a feeling of profound trust. In the absence of such trust, being understood is terrifying: the person who understands is an other, an entirely separate person who lives outside of one's control, and at the same time knows one to the core and could, if he chose, cut one to the quick. An effort to deaden oneself—for example, by dissociation, manic defense, foreclosure of psychic elaboration of experience by means of somatization or perversion—"would make sense" in that the core of one's being is at stake and needs to be protected in any way one has available.

As I have become more focused on these differences between explanation and understanding, I have noticed how the question "Why?" invites the patient to respond by drawing on the most conscious aspects of his personality (rooted in secondary process, cause-and-effect logic). By contrast, the question "What did it feel like?" invites a metaphorical *description*, which usually entails a much richer, emotion-laden response derived from more unconscious aspects of the personality.

I often ask myself what I think I am doing with patients with whom I am working in analysis. A response to this question that has become increasingly compelling to me in recent years is the idea that each patient brings to analysis—almost always without the words and ideas with which to state it—the feeling that he or she has, in an important sense, died in infancy or childhood, or perhaps at a later stage of life—and hopes that work with the analyst will help him or her to reclaim his or her "unlived life" (Ogden, 2014). As will be discussed in Chapter 3, the source of the psychic death is very often a set of events in infancy and childhood that involved the experience of "primitive agonies" (Winnicott, [1971] 1974) that were more than the patient could bear. In the face of terrifying events, the patient absents himself from his life and, in so doing, protects himself from massive psychic breakdown and a state of chronic psychosis. The patient, under these circumstances, reflexively protects himself by generating a psychic state in which the unbearable events are not experienced and instead persist as "unlived life." The individual is forever attempting to develop a personality system capable of containing the unbearable experience he has not lived. In the analytic setting, such a personality system is generated by the conjunction of the unconscious mind of patient and analyst. The creation of such a personality system is, to my mind, one way of conceiving of a fundamental goal of psychoanalysis.

We all have unlived aspects of our lives derived from early life events that were too painful for us to experience. These unlived events remain with us in the form of limitations in our personalities. We can feel these limitations in many ways, including the ways we feel constrained in the generosity and compassion and love we are capable of offering our spouse, our children, our parents, our friends, our patients, our students, as well as those whom we do not know, whom we have the power to help were we able to find it in ourselves to give assistance. I believe we are all the time engaged in unconscious psychological work in the act of dreaming—both while awake and asleep, both on our own and with others—that is of help to us in becoming better able to encompass formerly unlived aspects of our lives.

I will now try to clinically ground some of the ideas I have been discussing in this chapter, for ideas alone are insufficient to convey analytic understandings. *Description* of our clinical work is the most powerful tool we, as analysts, have in making our ideas accessible to others.

The five-sessions-per-week analysis with Mr. V had been troubling me for some time. I had grown to feel uneasy as I began most sessions. About a year into the analysis, I had a vivid dream in which I was with a group of people who were fleeing for reasons that were vague but terrifying; we had done something terrible, perhaps committed a murder. The police were cornering us and intended to either kill us or imprison us. I then found myself alone holding a loaded pistol as one of the policemen, who seemed hardly older than a boy, came charging toward me. I was struck by the fact that he was not protecting himself. He was not carrying a shield or wearing a bulletproof vest; he was not even carrying a baton, much less a gun. I pointed the pistol directly at his chest, but did not want to shoot him. As I was agonizingly trying to decide whether to pull the trigger, I woke up with my heart pounding.

When I met Mr. V in the waiting room the following morning, the dream came to mind, but the connection with him was unclear. In the course of the session, he mentioned his younger brother by name for the first time. He had often spoken of his sister, using her name, but had said very little about his brother, Paul.

Mr. V told me that Paul had called yesterday. "It's always upsetting to talk to him. It isn't actually having a conversation with anyone. He talks a mile a minute and I just listen. I can't understand most of what he's talking about."

The patient told me that Paul had been a very bright, artistic boy, but had what was diagnosed as a schizophrenic breakdown during his freshman year of college. He had never married, nor had he held a job for more than a few months at a time. He lived on welfare checks supplemented by money their parents gave him.

As I listened, Mr. V's description of his younger brother reminded me of the young policeman (a boy) in my dream whom I felt I had to kill or he would kill me or imprison me.

At this point in the session, I became upset at the thought of the interventions I had been making in recent sessions. They seemed, as I recalled them, to be not only premature, but badly missing the mark (that is, not feeling true to the experience of a given moment of a session, for which I had no words). It occurred to me that I had made these interventions in an effort to disguise (from myself and the patient) the fact that I felt lost in the analysis. "Lost" was a word that felt true to what I was feeling. Mr. V relied heavily on a certain way of relating to me when he felt lost, I thought. He regularly spoke to me as if I had no knowledge of literature, music, film, theater, or any other art form.

As these thoughts and feelings were going through my mind, Mr. V was silent for a few minutes, which was unusual for him. He then said, "I don't know why I feel responsible for Paul. I was at a different college from the one where he fell apart. I only found out about it after he was hospitalized. They moved him to a mental hospital in the middle of nowhere. So I couldn't visit him. That's not true, I could have visited, but I didn't want to see him in a mental hospital."

I asked, "Why not?" I regretted having asked this question as soon as the words came from my mouth. At this moment in the session, I felt deeply disturbed by the fact that I had not protected the patient from a confrontation that I delivered in the form of a question. It seemed to me that I must fear that truth as much as the patient did, though for reasons of my own. I felt as if I had awoken to a dimension of what was happening between the patient and me, though the nature of what I was sensing was still unclear. The session felt alive in a way that was new despite my unconscious effort to evade what was nascent at that moment in the analysis. It seems to me in retrospect that the psychological work done in "my dream" (which was, in a sense, a dream dreamt also by the patient) contributed to the psychological movement in the session. I felt far more compassionate toward Mr. V than I had in the past. I had viewed his condescension toward me as efforts to shore up his self-esteem. It now seemed to me that the patient was protecting himself from something far more dangerous a truth that he had for a very long time feared would kill him: the existance of his brother, whom he had all but banned from the analysis, until that session. What felt most real at that juncture was not a view that Mr. V was afraid of being saddled with his brother; rather, there was a sense of "rightness" to my feeling that Mr. V was trying to tell me, and very frightened of telling me, that he, like his brother, had had a breakdown in childhood from which he had never recovered. It was that part of himself that he had tried without success to keep out of the analysis. On the basis of all that had occurred in our first year of work together, it seemed to me that the patient's breakdown, unlike his brother's, had not been noticed or responded to. "They"—his parents, teachers, relatives, and other adults—had allowed themselves not to see who the patient was and not to respond to with recognition and understanding that he so badly needed. "They" did not know what was happening with him (and perhaps did not want to know)—just as he saw me as knowing nothing about literature, music, and so on, and just as the boy and I, in "my dream," were absolutely alone in the face of matters of life-and-death importance (to "lose one's mind" is to lose oneself, which is equivalent to losing one's life).

I was still getting my bearings as Mr. V, after another long pause, replied to my question, "Why not?" (Why hadn't he visited his brother when he was hospitalized?), by saying, "I'm ashamed to say that I was afraid of getting roped into some kind of family therapy with him where I'd have to hear about how important I was to him, and that I'd failed him as his big brother, and would have to save him now."

Turning on the couch toward the wall, he continued, "There's a part I don't want to tell you, but I know I'm supposed to say everything that's on my mind."

I asked, "How did you come to that idea?"

"That's one of the rules, isn't it?"

"It's one of your rules."

"So what are the rules here?"

"Why don't you have the right to say what you want to say to me, and keep to yourself what you want to keep to yourself?"

Mr. V was again quiet for quite a long time. It seemed to me he was having difficulty genuinely taking in the idea that he had a right to protect himself. In retrospect, I think that Mr. V had been confused by my intrusive question, "Why not?" In part he wanted very badly to face the truth of his breakdown, and unconsciously wanted my help in doing so; and at the same time, he felt that facing that truth alone would be the end of him. My question was confusing, I think, because it felt to Mr. V (and to me) as if I were distancing myself from him (particularly from the threat to his life that he felt the truth posed), and in so doing, I was leaving him alone, as (I sensed) he had been left alone with his breakdown in childhood. At the same time, I think that he also unconsciously sensed that I had changed (and had been changed by) the effect of my question on him and on me.

Space in this chapter does not allow for a detailed description of what unfolded in this analysis, but what I have said may provide a sense of the interplay of a need for truth, a fear of the truth, and the work that Mr. V and I put into living together an evolving understanding of what was occurring between us.

As I look at my life at present, as I write this chapter, I feel very fortunate that it has not been necessary for me to choose among what have become the passions of my life: the experience of practicing psychoanalysis; writing works expressing how I conceive of psycho-analytic theory and practice; writing other pieces in which I try to capture how I read particular poems and stories that hold profound importance to me; writing fiction; and, not by any means least of all, teaching both psychoanalysis and creative writing in seminars and consultation. To a significant degree, these forms of experience, taken together, are who I am, and therefore what I bring to patients, students, and colleagues.

I have grown up and grown old with my patients and students and perhaps have become a bit wiser in the process. As a consequence of the unusual intimacy that psychoanalysis, and often teaching, entails, I have many loves in my life. Most important, I have had the chance to live with patients their disturbing life events that they had not yet lived, and have marveled at the courage they have shown in attempting to do so.

Perhaps the pieces of this effort to say who I have become and am becoming as a psychoanalyst might be tied together by saying that I have found that what suits me best in my way of being a psychoanalyst is working at the frontier of yet to be known truths of human experience, a place that is constantly engendering wonder and humility.

★ ★ ★

My goal in bringing the chapters of this book together is to invite the reader not only to listen to the voices of these essays as they talk to one another, but to participate in that conversation, to create something new, something uniquely his or her own.

References

Bion, W. R. (1962a). Learning from experience. In *Seven servants*. New York: Aronson, 1977.

Bion, W. R. (1962b). A theory of thinking. In *Second thoughts* (pp. 110–119). New York: Aronson, 1967.

Freud, S. (1912). Recommendations to physicians practising psychoanalysis. *S. E.,* 12.

Freud, S. (1917). Mourning and melancholia. *S. E.,* 14 (pp. 242-258).

Grotstein, J. S. (2007). *A beam of intense darkness: Wilfred Bion's legacy to psychoanalysis.* London: Karnac.

Loewald, H. (1979). The waning of the Oedipus complex. In *Papers on psychoanalysis* (pp. 384–404). New Haven, CT: Yale University Press, 1980.

Ogden, T. H. (1994). The analytic third: Working with intersubjective clinical facts. *International Journal of Psychoanalysis*, 75, 3–20.

Ogden, T. H. (1995). Analysing forms of aliveness and deadness of the transference-countertransference. *International Journal of Psychoanalysis*, 76, 695–710.

Ogden, T. H. (1996). Reconsidering three aspects of psychoanalytic technique. *International Journal of Psychoanalysis*, 77, 883–899.

Ogden, T. H. (1997a). Reverie and interpretation. *Psychoanalytic Quarterly*, 66, 567–595.

Ogden, T. H. (1997b). Reverie and metaphor: Some thoughts on how I work as a psychoanalyst. *International Journal of Psychoanalysis*, 78, 719–732.

Ogden, T. H. (2004). This art of psychoanalysis: Dreaming undreamt dreams and interrupted cries. *International Journal of Psychoanalysis*, 85, 857–877.

Ogden, T. H. (2007). On talking-as-dreaming. *International Journal of Psychoanalysis*, 88, 575–589.

Ogden, T. H. (2009). Rediscovering psychoanalysis. In *Rediscovering psychoanalysis: Thinking and dreaming, learning and forgetting* (pp. 1–13). London: Routledge.

Ogden, T. H. (2010). Why read Fairbairn? *International Journal of Psychoanalysis*, 91, 101–118.

Ogden, T. H. (2014). Fear of breakdown and the unlived life. *International Journal of Psychoanalysis*, 95, 205–224.

Symington, N. (1983). The analyst's freedom to think as agent of therapeutic change. *International Review of Psychoanalysis*, 10, 283–291.

Winnicott, D. W. (1945). Primitive emotional development. In *Through paediatrics to psycho-analysis* (pp. 145–156). New York: Basic Books.

Winnicott, D. W. (1971/1974). Fear of breakdown. In C. Winnicott, R. Shepherd, and M. Davis eds, *Psychoanalytic explorations* (pp. 87–95). Cambridge, MA: Harvard University Press, 1989.

2

ON THREE FORMS OF THINKING

Magical thinking, dream thinking, and transformative thinking

In broad strokes, the current era of psychoanalysis might be thought of as the era of thinking about thinking. It seems to me that many of the most interesting and generative questions with which analysts are currently working have less to do with the symbolic content of dreams, associations, play, and other behavior, and more to do with what work we do psychically with our lived experience. In other words, our attention as analytic clinicians and analytic theorists has been increasingly focused on *the way* a person thinks, as opposed to *what* he thinks. To my mind, the two most important contributors to this movement in psychoanalysis are Winnicott, who attended more to the capacity for playing than to the symbolic content of play; and Bion, who explored in his writing the process of dreaming/thinking far more extensively than he discussed the symbolic meanings of dreams and associations.

In this chapter, I will demonstrate some of the ways in which this shift in emphasis from symbolic content to thought process has altered the ways I approach my analytic work.

I conceive of the three forms of thinking that I will be discussing—magical thinking, dream thinking, and transformative thinking—as coexisting, mutually creating, preserving, and negating aspects of every experience of

thinking. None of these forms of thinking is ever encountered in pure form.[1]
Neither is there a linear relationship among these forms of thinking,
such as a "progression" from magical thinking to dream thinking. Rather, I see these forms of thinking as standing in dialectical
tension with one another, just as I view the relationship between
the conscious and unconscious mind; the paranoid-schizoid, the
depressive, and the autistic-contiguous positions (Klein, 1946; Ogden,
1989); the psychotic and the nonpsychotic parts of the personality
(Bion, 1957); the basic assumption groups and the work group (Bion,
1959); the container and the contained (Bion, 1970); primary and
secondary process thinking (Freud, 1911); and so on. *Moreover, none
of these forms of thinking is a single, unitary way of thinking; rather, each
"form of thinking" represents a rather wide spectrum of ways of thinking.
The particular variation of the form of thinking that an individual may employ
is always in flux and depends upon his level of psychological maturity, the
intrapsychic and interpersonal emotional context of the moment, cultural factors,
and so forth.*

The forms of thinking upon which I will focus by no means
encompass the entire spectrum of ways of thinking. For example, I
will not address operational thinking (de M'Uzan, 1984, 2003),
autistic thinking (Tustin, 1981), psychic foreclosure (McDougall,
1984), or "phantasy in the body" (Gaddini, 1969), to name only a
few.

In order to provide a sense of the trajectory of this chapter, I will
briefly introduce the three forms of thinking before delving into each
clinically and theoretically. (In the tradition of Bion, when I speak
of *thinking*, I am always referring to thinking and feeling.) I use the
term *magical thinking* to refer to thinking that relies on omnipotent
fantasy to create a psychic reality that the individual experiences as
"more real" than external reality—for example, as seen in the use of
the manic defense. Such thinking substitutes invented reality for actual
external reality, thereby maintaining the existing structure of the
internal world. Moreover, magical thinking subverts the opportunity
to learn from one's lived experience with real external objects. The
psychological cost paid by the individual for his reliance on magical

---

1 Of the inseparability of forms of thinking, Freud (1900) wrote: "It is true that,
   so far as we know, no psychical apparatus exists which possesses a primary process
   only [i.e., without secondary process] and that such an apparatus is to that extent
   a theoretical fiction" (p. 603).

thinking is a practical one: magical thinking does not work in the sense that nothing can be built on it except for additional layers of magical constructions.

I use the term *dream thinking* to refer to the thinking we do in the process of dreaming. It is our most profound form of thinking, which continues both while we are asleep and in waking life. Though it is primarily an unconscious mental activity, it acts in concert with preconscious and conscious thinking. In dream thinking, one views and attributes meaning to experience simultaneously from multiple vantage points—for example, from the perspectives of primary and of secondary process thinking, of the container and of the contained, of the infantile self and of the mature self, and so on (Bion, 1962a; Grotstein, 2009). Dream thinking generates genuine psychological growth. Such thinking may be done on one's own, but a point is inevitably reached beyond which one needs another person with whom to think/dream one's most deeply troubling emotional experience.

The third of the forms of thinking that I will discuss, *transformative thinking*, is a form of dream thinking that involves a radical alteration of the terms by which one orders one's experience: one transcends the categories of meaning that have previously been felt to be the only possible categories with which to organize one's experience. In transformative thinking, one creates new ways of ordering experience in which not only new meanings, but new types of feeling, forms of object relatedness, and qualities of emotional and bodily aliveness are generated. Such a fundamental change in one's way of thinking and experiencing is more striking in work with severely disturbed patients, but occurs in work with the full spectrum of patients.

In the course of the discussion that follows, I will present clinical examples that illustrate some of the ways in which conceptualizing forms of thinking in the ways I have described is of value to me in talking with myself—and, at times, with the patient—about what I think is occurring in the analytic relationship and in other sectors of the patient's internal life and life in the world.

Magical thinking

Beginning with Freud (1909, 1913), omnipotent thought has been a well-established concept in psychoanalytic theory. Freud (1913) credits the Rat Man with coining the term *omnipotence of thought* (p. 85). I will make a few observations that capture something of

19

my sense of the differences between magical thinking and the other two forms of thinking that I explore in this chapter.

Magical thinking has one purpose and one purpose only: to evade facing the truth of one's internal and external experience. The method employed to achieve this end is the creation of a state of mind in which the individual believes that he creates the reality in which he and others live. Under such circumstances, psychic reality eclipses external reality: reality is "the reality not of experience but of thought" (Freud, 1913, p. 86). Consequently, emotional surprise and encounters with the unexpected are, as much as possible, foreclosed. In the extreme, when the individual fears that the integrity of the self is in danger, he may defend himself by means of virtually all-encompassing omnipotent fantasies that so disconnect him from external reality that his thinking becomes delusional and/or hallucinatory. In this psychological state, the individual is unable to learn from experience and incapable of distinguishing between being awake and being asleep (Bion, 1962a)—i.e., he is psychotic.

To the degree that psychic reality eclipses external reality, there is a progressive deterioration of the individual's capacity to differentiate dreaming and perceiving, symbol and symbolized. As a result, consciousness itself (self-awareness) is compromised or lost. This leads to a state of affairs in the analytic setting in which the patient treats his thoughts and feelings not as subjective experiences, but as facts.

Magical thinking underlies a great many psychological defenses, feeling states, and forms of object relatedness. I will briefly discuss only three. Mania and hypomania reflect the hegemony of a set of omnipotent fantasies: the individual relying on the manic defense feels that he has absolute control over the missing object, and therefore he has not lost the object, he has rejected it; he celebrates, not grieves, the loss of the object because he is better off without it; and the loss is not a loss because the object is valueless and contemptible. The feeling states associated with these omnipotent fantasies are concisely summed up by Klein (1935) as feelings of control, contempt, and triumph.

Projective identification is also based upon omnipotent fantasy: the unconscious belief that one can split off dangerous and endangered aspects of oneself and put them into another person in such a way that that aspect of oneself takes control of the other person from within. (The act of "containing" [Bion, 1970; Ogden, 2004a] a projective identification involves the "recipient's" transforming the "projector's" magical thinking into dream thinking, which the projector may be able to utilize in dreaming/thinking his own experience.)

Similarly, envy (which protects the individual from disturbing feelings, such as abject emptiness and desolation) involves the omnipotent fantasy that one is able to steal what one lacks from another person and spoil what remains of what is envied in that person.

The qualities of magical thinking just discussed all reflect the use of omnipotent fantasy in the service of creating the illusion (and, at times, delusion) that one is not subject to the laws that apply to others, including the laws of nature, the inescapability of time, the role of chance, the irreversibility of death, and so on. One may speak cruelly to another person and then believe that one can literally "take back" the comment (re-create reality—for instance, by renaming it a joke). Saying something makes it so. One's words are felt to have the power to substitute a newly created reality for a reality that is no longer convenient. More broadly, history can be rewritten at will.

Magical thinking is very convenient—simply saying something obviates the need to face the truth of what has occurred, much less do anything about it. But as convenient as magical thinking is, it has one overriding drawback: it does not "work"—nothing can be built on it or with it except additional layers of magical constructions. Such "thinking" has no traction in the real world that exists outside of one's mind. Rather than constituting a form of genuine thought, it is an attack both on the recognition of reality and on thinking itself (i.e., it is a form of anti-thinking). It substitutes invented reality for actual reality, thus collapsing the difference between internal and external reality. The belief, for example, that one can use an indiscriminate "forgive-and-forget" approach to interpersonal experience serves not only to further blind the individual to the reality of the nature of the emotional connection that exists between himself and others, but also further blinds him to who he himself is. He increasingly becomes a fiction—a magical invention of his own mind, a construction divorced from external reality.

Nothing (and no one) can be built on or with magical thinking because omnipotently created "reality" lacks the sheer immovable alterity of actual external reality. The experience of the otherness of external reality is necessary for the creation of genuine self-experience. If there is no *not-I*, there can be no *I*. Without a differentiated other, one is everyone and no one.

One implication of this understanding of the central role of the recognition of otherness in the development of the self is the idea that, as important as it is for the analyst to understand the patient, it is equally important for the analyst to be a person who is different from the patient. The last thing in the world any patient needs is a second version of himself. The solipsistic aspects of a patient's thinking—the self-reinforcing nature of his ties to his unconscious beliefs—leads to a limitation of the patient's ability to think and to grow psychologically. What the patient (unconsciously) is asking of the analyst—even when the patient is explicitly or implicitly claiming that he has no need of the analyst—is a conversation with a person other than himself, a person who is grounded in a reality that the patient has not created (see Fairbairn, 1944; Ogden, 2010).

A patient who was reduced to omnipotence[2]

Ms. Q told me in the initial interview that she had come to me for analysis because "I am unusually talented in wrecking everything in my life—my marriage, the way I treat my children, and the way I do my work." Despite the intended irony of this statement, it felt to me to be more a boast than an admission of failure or a request for help. It seemed to me that Ms. Q was putting me on notice that she was no ordinary person ("I am unusually talented").

In the first week of Ms. Q's five-sessions-per-week analysis, something quite striking occurred. Ms. Q left a phone message saying that, due to a change in her work schedule, she was unable to attend the meeting we had scheduled for the following day, but she would be able to attend the session just after the one we had scheduled, i.e., she could meet an hour later. She ended the message by saying, "I'll assume that's all right with you unless I hear from you." I had no choice but to return her phone call. In my phone message, I said that I expected her at the time we had agreed upon. Had I not returned her call, she would have arrived at the same time as the patient to whom that later session belonged, which would have

---

2 Bion once said to his analysand, James Grotstein, "What a shame it was that you were reduced to omnipotence" (Grotstein, 2001). The connection between shame and omnipotent thinking that Bion subtly makes in this comment is a highly significant one: unconscious, irrational shame is a powerful force impelling one to give up on the real world and instead create a world that is fully under one's control.

created an intrusive situation for the other patient and me when the three of us met in the waiting room.

The patient arrived twenty minutes late for the session she had asked to change. She offered facile apologies and explanations. I said to her, "It seems to me that you don't believe I've genuinely made a place for you here and so you feel you have to steal one. But I don't think that such things can be stolen." I strongly suspected that the fear of not having a place of her own had been a lifelong anxiety for the patient, but I did not say this to her.

Ms. Q said that she did not think it was so complicated as that, and went on to tell me more about events at work. I said to her, "I guess I'm not to have a place here with you unless I fight for it." The patient behaved as if I had said nothing.

Ms. Q spoke in a rather flippant way about her life. In talking about her "formative years," she said that she had had a "perfectly normal childhood" and had "perfectly reasonable parents" who were highly successful academics. "I can't blame it all on them." I imagined that what the patient said was true in a way that she was not at all aware of. That is, she had been a "perfectly" behaved child (compliant, and fearful of her emotions), and her parents were "perfectly reasonable" in the sense that they were little able to be receptive to, or expressive of, feeling. This inference was borne out over time, both in the transference-countertransference and in the patient's accounts of her childhood.

Closely linked with Ms. Q's efforts to control me and steal from me and from my other patients was her belief that I had the answers to her problems—her inability to be a mother, a wife, a friend, or a productive member of her profession. My "stubbornness" in not giving her solutions to her problems puzzled and enraged her.

I gradually became aware of a way in which the patient had been relating to me from the very beginning of the analysis, but which had become less disguised and more provocative as time went on. The patient would regularly misrepresent feelings, behaviors, and events that had occurred either within or outside of the consulting room. This was most striking when Ms. Q distorted something that she or I had said in the current session or in a recent one. After almost two years of feeling controlled in this way, I said, "I think that by presenting yourself and me with story after story that you know to be untrue or misleadingly incomplete, you ensure that everything I say or think is of no interest or value to you. Reality is only a story that you create and re-create as you choose. There is no real me or real you that lies outside of your control. Since you can create any reality that suits you, there's no need to actually do anything to make the changes in your life that you say you want to make."

As I said this to Ms. Q, I was aware that I was angry at her for the ways she undermined me and the analytic work. I was also aware that my pointing out that she was failing to conduct herself in a way that I approved of would likely force her into an even more highly defended state. (That is, in fact, what ensued.) But it was not my anger that was most disturbing to me at this point. I was speaking in a chastising way that felt quite foreign to me.

A few sessions later, I closed my eyes for a few minutes while sitting in my chair behind the couch (as I often do while working with patients in analysis). After a while, I suddenly became very anxious. I opened my eyes, but for a few moments did not know where I was, what I was doing, or whom, if anyone, I was with. My disorientation did not lift even after I saw a person lying on the couch. It took me a few seconds more to deduce where I was, who the person on the couch was, and what I was doing there (i.e., who I was). It took several more moments before this deductive thinking was succeeded by a more solid sense of myself as a person and as Ms. Q's analyst. This was a disquieting experience that led me, over time, to become aware of my own fears of losing myself in the psychological-interpersonal experience in which Ms. Q continuously reinvented reality and reinvented herself and me. It seemed to me that Ms. Q was showing me what she could not tell me (or herself), i.e., what it felt like to invent and reinvent herself, and to be invented and reinvented by another person. I was reminded of Ms. Q's parents' demand on her, and her own efforts to be "a perfect child," a child who makes no emotional demands on her parents, a child who is not a child.

I said to Ms. Q, "I think that your distortions of reality, and particularly your inventions of yourself and me, are efforts to show me what you don't feel able to convey to me in words. It seems to me that when you were a child, you felt you were the invention of someone else's mind, and you continue to feel that way. I think that you've been afraid to tell me or to tell yourself the truth because that would endanger what little you have of yourself that feels real. To tell me the truth would be to leave yourself open to my taking from you what feels most real about you, and replacing it with my own version of you." Ms. Q did not reflexively dismiss what I said with a sardonic quip or other form of contemptuous dismissal, as was her wont. Instead, she was quiet for the few minutes that remained of the hour.

In the following day's session, Ms. Q told me a dream: "I was playing tennis—in reality I don't know how to play tennis—and the ball rolled to a far corner of the series of courts on which we were playing. There was a kind of trough at the edge of the far court that was filled with brand-new tennis balls, but I didn't know how to take more than one or two with me. I can't remember what happened after that. I woke up in the morning feeling all right—not great, not terrible."

I said, "In telling the dream, you told me and yourself right away that in the dream you are playing tennis, but in reality you can't play tennis. It seems that it felt important to you that we both know what is real and what isn't. The ball rolled to a far corner where there's a trough. You find a great many new tennis balls in it—it seems like an exciting treasure, but you can only take one or two with you. On the other hand, the tennis balls that you already have are enough. When you woke up, you didn't feel cheated of a treasure, nor did you feel like a thief, as you have felt so often in the past. You felt all right."

Ms. Q said, "That's right, I didn't really care that I couldn't take all the tennis balls. I didn't want them or need them. Finding the tennis balls in the trough didn't feel like discovering a treasure, it just seemed strange. When I was a kid . . . actually I was in high school . . . I shoplifted things I didn't want and threw them away as soon as I got outside the store. It makes me feel queasy remembering that. I knew I didn't want the stuff, but I couldn't stop myself."

In the course of the succeeding year of analysis, Ms. Q's creation of her own reality greatly diminished. At times, when she was engaged in distorting reality, she would interrupt herself, saying, "If I continue talking in this way, it will be pointless because I'm leaving out an important part of what happened that I'm embarrassed to tell you."

In the portions of the analysis that I have discussed, the patient relied heavily on magical thinking in an effort to create (and destroy) reality, including herself and me. The alternative to creating reality, for her, was not simply an experience of helplessness, but a sense of losing herself, a feeling of having herself stolen by someone else. Moreover, she felt ashamed of not being able to hold onto a sense of herself that felt real and true to her.

The patient's distortions of reality (her magical creation of her own reality) angered me because of the way in which they contributed to what felt like a theft of meaning from the analytic dialogue and a theft of my sense of self. What I initially said to the patient regarding her magical thinking was excessively accusatory and, consequently, unutilizable by her. It was, however, of value to me in alerting me to the way in which I did not recognize myself in the way I was talking. This understanding, in turn, created a psychological space in which a reverie experience was generated (by the patient and me) in which I experienced a frightening feeling that I did not know who I was, where I was, or who was with me.

Talking with Ms. Q about what I believed to be her feelings of losing herself in her endless reinventions of reality provided an emotional context (a containing way of thinking) that allowed her to dream (with me) an experience of being herself in the world without the need for magic. The patient, both in the tennis ball dream and in talking with me about it, was able to be accepting of herself as she was. Reality was not a threat; it served as a grounding otherness. My otherness and the otherness of external reality were made more immediately present as I "retold" the tennis ball dream in a form that was other to her own telling of it. In hearing my telling of the dream, Ms. Q, I believe, saw something like herself (herself at an observable distance) in "my dream." The patient made use of the external reality (the otherness) of my version of the dream in a self-defining way, as reflected in her quietly correcting my version of the dream in places where she felt she did not recognize herself. For example, she told me that finding the multitude of tennis balls "didn't feel like discovering a treasure"; rather, she found it "strange" (that is, foreign to the person whom she was becoming).

While this section of the chapter has focused on magical thinking, the work of coming to understand something of what was occurring in the analytic relationship involved a good deal of dream thinking on both the patient's part and mine. I will further describe this aspect of the analysis in the next section of this chapter. (As I mentioned earlier, one's thinking always involves the full spectrum of forms of thinking. What varies is the prominence of one form, or combination of forms, at any given moment.)

Dream thinking

Dream thinking is the predominantly unconscious psychological work that we do in the course of dreaming. We dream continually, both while we are awake and while we are asleep (Bion, 1962a).

Just as the light of the stars in the sky is obscured by the glare of the sun during the day, dreaming continues while we are awake, though it is obscured by the glare of waking life. Dream thinking is our most encompassing, penetrating, and creative form of thinking. We are insatiable in our need to dream our lived experience in an effort to create personal, psychological meanings (which are organized and represented in such forms as visual images, verbal symbols, kinesthetically organized impressions, and so on) (Barros and Barros, 2008).

In dream thinking, we view our lived experience from a multiplicity of vantage points simultaneously, which allows us to enter into a rich, nonlinear set of unconscious conversations with ourselves about our lived experience. That multitude of vantage points includes the perspectives of primary and secondary process thinking; the container and the contained; the paranoid-schizoid, depressive, and autistic-contiguous positions (Ogden, 1989); the mature self and the infantile self; the magical and the real; the "psychotic" and "nonpsychotic" parts of the personality (Bion, 1957); getting to know what one is experiencing (Bion's [1970] "K") and becoming the truth of what one is experiencing (Bion's [1970] "O"); the "projector" and the "recipient" of projective identification; and so on. The multilayered, nonlinear "conversations" constituting dream thinking take place between unconscious aspects of the personality, termed by Grotstein (2000) "the dreamer who dreams the dream" and "the dreamer who understands the dream," and by Sandler (1976) "the dream-work" and "the understanding work." Such thinking would result in massive confusion if it were to occur consciously while one was attempting to go about the business of waking life.

The richness of dream experience and dream thinking is captured by Pontalis (2003: pp. 15, 18, 19) in his description of waking up from sleep:

> I must separate myself brutally from the nocturnal world, from this world where I felt and lived more incidents than anywhere else, where I was extraordinarily active, where I was more awake than one ever is in what we call the "state of wakefulness."
>
> . . . [Dreams] think and they think for me. . . . Waking up we would like to recover the beautiful, distressing, and disturbing images that visited us in the night and already these images are fading. Yet we also feel that what we are losing then is much more than these images; it's a realm of thought that progresses continuously.

... [Dreaming] ... unaware of its destination ... [is] carried away
by the sole power of its movement.

As discussed earlier, the problem with magical thinking is the fact
that it does not work: it substitutes invented reality for the reality of
who one is and the emotional circumstances in which one is living.
Consequently, nothing of substance changes in oneself. The strength
of dream thinking lies in the fact that it does work: it does give rise
to psychological growth, as reflected, for instance, in the way one
consciously and unconsciously goes about making changes in the way
one relates to other people and in one's other engagements with the
real external world. In this sense, I view pragmatism as a principal
means of taking the measure of the value of any aspect of the
workings of the mind (as is true of the workings of the body). A
fundamental question regarding any given form of thinking is always:
Does it work? Does it contribute to the development of a sense of
an emotionally alive, creative, self-aware person, grounded in the
reality of both himself and of the external world?

Beginning in earliest infancy and continuing throughout life, every
individual is limited, to varying degrees, in his capacity to subject his
lived experience to dream thinking, i.e., to do unconscious
psychological work in the course of dreaming. When one has reached
the limits of one's ability to dream one's disturbing experiences, one
needs another person to help one dream one's undreamt dreams
(Ogden, 2004b, 2005). In other words, it takes (at least) two people
to dream one's most disturbing experience.

In earliest life, the psychological-interpersonal phenomenon that
I am describing takes the form of the mother and infant together
dreaming the infant's disturbing experience (as well as the mother's
emotional response to the infant's distress). The mother, in a state of
reverie, accepts the infant's unthinkable thoughts and unbearable
feelings (which are inseparable from her response to the infant's
distress) (Bion, 1962a, 1962b; Ogden, 1997a, 1997b). The mother,
who in this way enters into a subjectivity that is co-created with the
infant (Winnicott's [1956] "primary maternal preoccupation"; Bion's
[1962a] and Rosenfeld's [1987] "intrapsychic-interpersonal version
of projective identification"; Ferro's [1999] "bi-personal field"; or
what I call the "intersubjective third" [Ogden, 1994a, 1994b]), brings
to bear on the infant's unthinkable experience her own larger personality and greater capacity for dreaming. In so doing, she and the infant
together dream something like the infant's disturbing experience.

The mother communicates to the infant his formerly undreamable/ unthinkable experience in a form that he is now more fully able to dream on his own. A similar intersubjective process takes place in the analytic relationship and in other intimate relationships, such as the parent-child relationship, marriage, close friendships, and relationships between siblings.

In saying that it takes (at least) two people to think one's most disturbing emotional experience, I do not mean to say that individuals are not able to think on their own. Rather, I am saying that one inevitably reaches a point in one's thinking/dreaming beyond which one cannot go. At that juncture, one either develops symptomatology in an (often futile) effort to gain some measure of control over (which is not to say resolution of) one's psychological difficulties, or one enlists another person to help one dream one's experience. As Bion (1987) put it, "the human unit is a couple; it takes two human beings to make one" (p. 222).

It must be borne in mind that not all forms of mental activity that appear to be dreaming—for example, visual images and narratives experienced in sleep—merit the name *dreaming*. Post-traumatic nightmares that are repeated night after night achieve virtually no unconscious psychological work, and consequently do not constitute genuine dreaming (Bion, 1987). In other words, such "dreams" are dreams that are not dreams in that they leave the dreamer psychically unchanged. Again, the measure of whether a dream is a dream is whether it "works"—whether it facilitates real psychological change and growth.

The ordinary rescued from the magical

As I mentioned in connection with my work with Ms. Q, dream thinking was done at several critical points in that analysis. I will focus here on one of these instances: my use of my reverie experience that occurred during a session in which I listened to the patient while my eyes were closed. In that reverie, I was, in an important sense, dreaming *with* Ms. Q an experience that she had been unable to dream on her own (much less put into words for herself or for me). The reverie itself was a form of waking dreaming in which I not only lived the experience, but—even as I was in the grip of it—I was also able to form questions that addressed the essence of the emotional situation: Where am I? Who am I? With whom am I?

29

On "waking" from the reverie, I was able to engage in more conscious aspects of dream thinking. This involved my conceiving of my experience of having momentarily lost myself as constituting an unconsciously co-created version of Ms. Q's experience of losing herself as a consequence of her use of omnipotent fantasy to invent and reinvent herself and me.

The thinking I have just described involved apprehending and putting into words multiple levels of meaning that were alive in the emotional experience. I treated my reverie experience both as an experience of having co-created a dream with Ms. Q, and as an experience that had personal meanings that were unique to each of us. My own experience of the reverie was one in which I briefly lost touch with my sense of who I was, while Ms. Q's experience of losing herself was lifelong and at times quasi-delusional.

As I have said, I view dream thinking as a form of thinking that is primarily unconscious, although it operates in concert with preconscious and conscious thinking. The co-creation of the reverie experience itself was principally an unconscious phenomenon that generated preconscious and conscious imagery (as is the case with dreams that one remembers after waking from sleep). In relating my reverie experience to Ms. Q's experience of herself, I was primarily engaged in conscious, secondary process thinking, but that type of thinking would, I believe, have been stale and empty had I not been speaking *from* my experience as a participant in the reverie.

An important measure of whether or not the thinking that Ms. Q and I did was genuine dream thinking lies in the degree to which it facilitated the work of helping the patient become more alive and responsive to her experience in the real world, better able to accept herself as she was, and more capable of thinking and talking about her experience with herself and with me. It seems to me that my use of my reverie experience to talk with Ms. Q about *her* experience of losing herself reflected psychological change in me, i.e., in my own increased capacity to contain the patient's unthinkable/undream-able experience (as opposed to evacuating it—for example, in the form of a chastising intervention). My talking with Ms. Q about her experience of losing herself contributed, I believe, to her dreaming her tennis ball dream, a dream in which she had little interest in, or use for, magical thinking. Her psychological growth was reflec-ted in her capacity to dream that dream and in her enhanced ability to talk and think with me (and herself) about it.

The type of dream thinking that I have described here involved a form of self-reflection in which I drew my own experience, and my conception of the patient's experience, into relation to one another; i.e., I made use of my experience of losing myself to make an inference regarding the patient's experience of losing herself. The category of meaning (the experience of losing oneself) remained relatively constant. As will be seen in the following section of this chapter, dream thinking at times involves a radical shift in the structure of the patient's and the analyst's thinking. This form of dream thinking, which I refer to as *transformative thinking*, may precipitate what Bion (1970) refers to as "catastrophic change" (p. 106), a change in nothing less than everything.

Transformative thinking

The idea of transformative thinking occurred to me in response to a passage from the King James translation of the Gospel of John, which was discussed in an essay by Seamus Heaney (1986). I will treat the writing in that passage as a literary text, not a religious text, and therefore, I will treat the figures and events depicted in the story not as expressions of theological meaning, but as expressions of emotional truths arrived at by means of a particular form of thinking. Because the thinking is *in* the writing, I will quote the passage in its entirety:

> And the scribes and Pharisees brought unto him a woman taken in adultery; and when they had set her in the midst,
>
> They say unto him, Master, this woman was taken in adultery, in the very act.
>
> Now Moses in the law commanded us, that such should be stoned: but what sayest thou?
>
> This they said, tempting him, that they might have to accuse him. But Jesus stooped down, and with his finger wrote on the ground, as though he heard them not.
>
> So when they continued asking him, he lifted up himself, and said unto them, He that is without sin among you, let him first cast a stone at her.
>
> And again he stooped down, and wrote on the ground.
>
> And they which heard it, being convicted by their own conscience, went out one by one, beginning at the eldest, even unto the last: and Jesus was left alone, and the woman standing in the midst.

When Jesus had lifted up himself, and saw none but the woman, he said unto her, Woman, where are those thine accusers? hath no man condemned thee?

She said, No man, Lord. And Jesus said unto her, neither do I condemn thee: go, and sin no more.

(Gospel of John [8: 3–11])

In this story, Jesus is brought into a situation in which a woman has been taken "in the very act" of adultery. He is asked whether he will obey the law (which demands that the woman be stoned) or break the law (by putting a stop to the stoning that is about to take place).

Jesus, instead of replying to the question, "stooped down, and with his finger wrote on the ground as though he heard them not." Instead of accepting the terms as they were presented (Will you obey the law or break the law?), Jesus opens a psychological space in which to think in the act of writing. The reader is never told what he wrote. Jesus's writing on the ground breaks the powerful forward movement toward action and, in so doing, creates a space for thinking both for the characters in the story and for the reader/listener.

When Jesus stands, he does not reply to the question that has been posed. He says something utterly unexpected and does so in the simplest of words—a sentence in which all but two of the fifteen words are monosyllabic: "He that is without sin among you, let him first cast a stone at her." Jesus does not address the question of whether to obey the law or break the law, and instead poses a completely different, highly enigmatic question: How does one bring to bear one's own experience of being human, which includes one's own sinful acts, to the problem of responding to the behavior of another person? And, further, the passage raises the question of whether any person has the right to stand in judgment of another person. At the end of the passage, Jesus renounces any intention of standing in judgment of the woman: "Neither do I condemn thee."

The final words of the passage: "go, and sin no more," are tender, while at the same time, demand honest self-scrutiny. Language itself has been altered: the meaning of the word *sin* has been radically transformed in the course of the story, but into what? In relation to what moral order is sin to be defined? Is the woman free to commit adultery if her own morality does not deem it a sin? Are all systems of morality equal in their capacity to prescribe, proscribe, and take the measure of the way human beings conduct themselves in relation to themselves and one another?

My purpose in discussing this piece of literature is to convey what I mean by transformative thinking. It is a form of dream thinking that involves recognizing the limitations of the categories of meaning currently thought to be the only categories of meaning (e.g., obey the law or break the law), and, in their place, creating fundamentally new categories—a radically different way of ordering experience—that had been unimaginable up to that point.

The biblical story I have just discussed constitutes one of the most important narratives—and instances of transformative thinking—of the past 2,000 years. No doubt it would have been forgotten long ago had it been less enigmatic, less irreducible to other terms (such as the tenets of a new set of secular or religious laws to be obeyed or disobeyed), or even to abstract principles such as: no person has the right to pass judgment on another person. Had the story merely substituted one binary choice for another, or introduced a new pre-scription, the thinking achieved in the writing would not have been transformative in nature and, I speculate, would not have survived as a seminal narrative of Western culture. The story, like a poem, cannot be paraphrased and mined for meanings that stand still.

We, as psychoanalysts, ask of ourselves and of our patients no less than transformative thinking, even as we recognize how difficult it is to achieve. Our theoretical and clinical work becomes stagnant if at no point do we engage in transformative thinking. It is this striving for transformative thinking that makes psychoanalysis a subversive activity, an activity inherently undermining of the gestalt (the silent, self-defining terms) of the intrapsychic, the interpersonal, and the social cultures in which patient and analyst live.

Each of the major twentieth-century analytic theorists has introduced his or her own conception of the transformation—the alteration of the way we think and experience being alive—that is most central for psychological growth. For Freud (1900, 1909), it is making the unconscious conscious and, later in his work (1923, 1926, 1933), movement in psychic structure from id to ego ("Where id was, there ego shall be" [1933, p. 80]). For Klein (1948, 1952), the pivotal transformation is the movement from the paranoid-schizoid to the depressive position; for Bion (1962a), it is a movement from a mentality based on evacuation of disturbing, unmentalized emotional experience to a mentality in which one attempts to dream/think one's experience, and, later (1965, 1970), a movement from getting to know the reality of one's experience (K) to becoming the truth of one's experience (O). For Fairbairn (1944), therapeutic transformation involves a movement from life lived in relation to internal objects to a life lived in relation to real external objects. For Winnicott (1971), crucial to psychological health is the psychic transformation in which one moves from unconscious fantasying to a capacity to live imaginatively in an intermediate space between reality and fantasy.

My focus in this section of the present chapter is not on the validity or clinical usefulness of each of these conceptions of psychic transformation, but on the nature of the intrapsychic and intersubjective thinking/dreaming that mediates these transformations. As will be seen in the next clinical illustration that I will present, the achievement of transformative thinking is not necessarily an experience of a sudden breakthrough, a eureka phenomenon. Rather, in my experience, it is most often the outcome of years of slow, painstaking analytic work that involves an expanding capacity of the analytic pair to dream aspects of the patient's formerly undreamable experience.

Transformative thinking—thinking that radically alters the terms by which one orders one's experience—lies toward one end of a spectrum of degrees of change-generating thinking (dream thinking). The clinical example that follows is taken from work with a patient who experienced florid psychotic thinking, both prior to the analysis and in the course of the analysis. I have elected to discuss my work with this patient because the transformative thinking that was required of the patient and me is more apparent and more striking than in most of my work with healthier patients. Nonetheless, it must be borne in mind that transformative thinking is an aspect of all thinking and, as such, is a dimension of my work with the full spectrum of patients.

A woman who was not herself

Ms. R sat stiffly in her chair, unable to make eye contact with me during our first consultation session. She was well dressed but in a way that seemed artificial in its perfection. She began by saying, "I'm wasting your time. I don't think that what is wrong with me can change. I'm not a person who should be in an analyst's office." I said, "The first thing you want me to know about you is that you don't belong here. I think you're warning me that both of us will no doubt regret having had anything to do with one another."

Ms. R replied, "That's right." After a minute or so, she said, "I should tell you something about myself." I said, "You can do that if you like, but you're already telling me, in your own way, a great deal about who you feel you are and what frightens you most."

Space does not allow for a discussion of the initial years of analysis. In brief, Ms. R spoke with great shame and embarrassment about how repulsive she felt; she continually readied herself for my telling her to leave. As we talked about these feelings, the patient slowly became more trusting of me. In a very unassuming way, Ms. R revealed herself to be a highly intelligent, articulate, and likable person.

Toward the end of the third year of this five-sessions-per-week analysis, Ms. R said, "There's something I'm afraid to tell you because you might tell me that I'm too sick to be in analysis. But you won't be able to help me if you don't know this about me, so I'm going to tell you." Ms. R haltingly went on to say that she had had "a breakdown" when she was in her thirties while traveling in Europe. She was hospitalized for a month, during which time she had a hallucination that lasted for several days. "In it, a string was coming out of my mouth. It's very hard for me to say this because I'm afraid of getting caught in it again. I was terrified and kept pulling on the string in order to get it out of me, but the string was endless. As I pulled, I found that my internal organs were attached to the string. I knew that if I didn't get this string out of me, I would die, but I also knew that if I pulled out more of the string, it would be the end of me because I couldn't live without my insides." Ms. R said that she had felt unbearably lonely during the hospitalization and was consumed by thoughts of suicide.

She and I talked at length about the hospitalization, the experiential level of the hallucination, and her fear that the hallucination would frighten and alienate me, and entrap her. I restricted myself to putting what she was saying into my own words in order to let her know that she was not alone now as she had been then. The hallucination seemed to me to be far too important an event to risk foreclosing it with premature understandings.

Ms. R also felt that I would have to know more about her childhood experience to be able to help her. She said, "I know I've been very vague in talking about my childhood and my parents. I'm sure you've noticed, but I couldn't bring myself to do it because it makes me feel physically ill to think about it. I don't want to get trapped there either." Ms. R said that, as a child, she had "worshipped" her mother: She was dazzlingly beautiful and extraordinarily intelligent, but I was as afraid of her as I was revering of her. I studied her way of walking, the way she held her head, the way she spoke to her friends, to the mailman, to the housekeeper. I wanted desperately to be like her, but I was never able to do it well enough. I could tell that she thought I was always falling short. She didn't need to say anything. It was unmistakable in the coldness of her eyes and in her tone of voice.

The patient's father was fully consumed with running the family business and was at home very little. Ms. R recalled lying in bed trying not to fall asleep so she might hear her father's voice and the sound of his movements around the house when he got home. She did not dare get out of bed for fear of displeasing her mother by "tiring her father out after his long day at work" (as her mother put it). Gradually, in the course of growing up, the patient came to understand that her mother could not tolerate sharing her father's attention. Her parents seemed to her, even as a child, to have had an unspoken agreement that her father could spend as much time at work as he wanted to, and in exchange her mother would run the house and the family as she pleased.

In this period of analytic work, the patient's lifelong, visceral sense of disgust for herself as a person and for her body (particularly its "female excretions") became so intense that Ms. R avoided as much as possible being around other people for fear that they would be repulsed by her odor. Being in my consulting room with me was almost unbearable for her. As she spoke about her "repulsive body" during one of these sessions, my mind wandered to a book that I was reading in which the narrator discussed the odor that clung to his own body and those of the other prisoners in the concentration camp in which he had spent more than a year. I thought, at that moment in the session, that not to be stained by the odor would have been far worse than being stained by it, because being free of the odor would have meant that one was a perpetrator of unthinkable atrocities. A prisoner's terrible odor obliterated his individual identity, but at least it served to mark the fact that he was not one of "them."

In talking with me about her revulsion for herself and her body, Ms. R gradually began to recognize the depth and severity of her mother's "distaste" for her. "It was as if being a child was an illness that my mother tried to cure me of. Only now do I see that her teaching me how to be 'a young woman of culture' was insane. I was able to convince myself that this was what mothers did. On my own, I learned how to rid myself of the [regional] accent with which the other children spoke."

When the patient's periods began at age twelve, her mother left a box of Kotex and a detailed letter about "how to keep yourself clean." Not a single spoken word passed between them on the subject. The patient's mother became significantly colder and more disapproving of Ms. R after the patient entered puberty.

After several more years during which the patient did considerable work with the understandings I have described, she began to experience left-sided abdominal pain that she was convinced was a symptom of cancer. When extensive medical tests failed to reveal a physiological source of the pain, the patient became extremely distressed and said, "I don't believe them. I don't believe their tests. They're not real doctors, they're researchers, not doctors." She then, for the first time in the analysis, sobbed deeply.

After a few minutes, I said, "It's terrifying to feel that doctors are not real doctors. You've put your life in their hands. But this is not a new experience for you. I think that you felt you had a mother who was not a real mother, and your life was completely in her hands. Just as you feel you are a guinea pig in the so-called doctors' research, I think that you felt you were merely a character in your mother's insane internal life."[3]

Ms. R listened to me intently, but did not respond in words to these comments. Her sobbing subsided and there was a visible decrease in the tension in her body as she lay on the couch.

The succeeding months of Ms. R's life, both within and outside the analysis, were deeply tormenting ones. During this period, she was again preoccupied with the string hallucination. The patient said she continued to feel the physical sensation of having her mother (who was now indistinguishable from the string) inside of her, though the sensory experience no longer held the unmediated realness of a hallucination. Ms. R came to view her fear (and conviction) that there

---

3 I also thought that Ms. R unconsciously experienced me as another doctor using her for my own purposes, perhaps as a subject for a lecture or paper, but I decided to wait to talk to her about that aspect of what I sensed was happening in the transference-countertransference until that set of thoughts and feelings was closer to her conscious experience of me. I believe that the patient would have experienced such a transference interpretation at that juncture as a substitution of my story for hers.

was a cancer growing inside of her as a new version of the string hallucination.

Also at this juncture in the analysis, Ms. R began to correct grammatical errors that I made—for instance, when I said, "people that" instead of "people who," or when I made an error in the use of the subjunctive. She subtly made her corrections by repeating the essence of my sentence, but with the error corrected. I am not sure whether the patient was at all aware that she was doing this. Ms. R openly complained about television news broadcasters and *The New York Times* "butchering the English language." I became highly self-conscious regarding the grammatical correctness of my speech, to the point that I felt tongue-tied and limited in my ability to speak in a spontaneous way. I was able, over time, to understand what was happening as the patient's way of unconsciously forcing me to experience something of what it felt like for her to have her imperious mother inside of her.

In a session in which Ms. R was feeling hopeless about ever being able to free herself of her mother's physical and emotional presence in her, I said, "I think that you feel today, almost as strongly as you did when you had the string hallucination, that you have only two choices: you can try to pull the string out of you—but that requires pulling out your own insides along with your mother, which would kill both of you. Or you can choose not to pull out the string, which means giving up your last chance to remove her from you. You would be giving up all hope of ever becoming a person separate from her."

While I was saying this, I had a strong sense of emerging from a psychic state in which I had felt inhabited by Ms. R in a strangulating way. Something quite new, and very welcome, was occurring between the two of us at this point in the session, though I was unable to put it into words or images for myself or the patient.

Ms. R said, "As you were speaking, I remembered something that plagued me when I was in junior high and high school. I lived in a world of looming disaster. For instance, I had to predict exactly—to the tenth of a gallon—how much gas the car would take at the gas station. I was convinced that if I was wrong, my mother or father would die. But worst of all, there was a question that I could not get out of my head. I haven't thought about this for years. The question was: if my family and I were in a boat that was sinking, and everyone would drown unless one person was thrown overboard, and it was up to me to decide which one was to go, whom would I choose? I knew immediately that I would choose to throw myself into the water, but that answer was a 'wrong answer'—it was against the rules. So I would begin again asking myself the same question, and that went on over and over and over, sometimes for months."

I said, "As a girl, you were too young to know that it was not the answer you came up with that was wrong or against the rules—it was the very fact that the question had to be asked that was 'wrong' in the sense that there was something terribly wrong going on in your life and in the life of your family. I think that you've felt virtually every moment of your life, from the time you were a small child, that you have to decide who to kill—yourself or your mother."

Ms. R replied, "It was too awful—impossible—as a child to allow myself to know any of this. It's been there as a feeling, but I didn't have words for it. I felt she was everything. I knew that if I got her out of me, it would kill her, and I didn't want that, but I had to get her out, I didn't want to die. I'm so confused. I feel as if I'm in a maze and there's no way out. I have to get out of here. I don't think I can stay."

I said, "The very first thing you wanted me to know about you in our initial meeting was that you and I didn't belong here together. Now I realize that, despite the fact that you couldn't put it into words, you were trying to protect both of us from yourself. If you allow me to help you, I'll be inside of you and you'll have to kill one or both of us. As a child, you were alone with that problem, but that's not true any longer."

Ms. R said, "There are times when I'm here that I know that there is a world made entirely differently from the one I've been living in. I'm embarrassed to say this—I can feel myself blushing—but it is a world in which you and I talk like this. I'm sorry I said it because I don't want to jinx it. I feel like such a little girl now. Forget I said anything." I said, "Your secret is safe with me." I had grown very fond of Ms. R by this point in the analysis, and she knew that.

It was only at this juncture, with the patient's help—her telling me she felt like a little girl—that I was able to put into words for myself something of the emotions I had sensed earlier in the session, and was now feeling with far greater intensity. I was experiencing Ms. R as the daughter I never had, a daughter with whom I was feeling a form of tenderness and a form of loss (as she grows up) that is unique to the tie between a father and daughter. This was not simply a new thought, it was a new way of experiencing myself and Ms. R; it was a way of feeling alive both lovingly and sadly that was new to me.

In the next session, Ms. R said, "Last night, I slept more deeply than I've slept in a very long time. It is as if space has opened up in every direction, even downward in sleep."

As the analysis progressed, Ms. R was able to experience types of feeling and qualities of human relatedness that were new to her: "All my life I've heard the word *kindness* being used by people, but I had no idea what the word meant. I knew I had never felt the feeling they were talking about. I now know what kindness feels like. I can feel your kindness toward me. I cry when I see a mother tenderly holding her baby in her arms or holding the hand of her child as they walk." She said she cried because she could now feel how little kindness she had been shown as a child. But more important, she thought, was the terrible sadness that she felt about having shown so little kindness to her own children. Ms. R had only occasionally spoken of her children up to this point in the analysis, despite the fact that all of them were having emotional difficulties.

Over time, the psychological-interpersonal shift that I have described became stabilized as a way of being and perceiving for Ms. R. The stability of the change was reflected in the following dream: "I was returning home from somewhere and I found that people had moved into my house. There was a whole group of them and they were in every room—they were cooking in the kitchen, watching TV in the living room, they were everywhere. I was furious, I yelled at them, 'Get the fuck out of here! [I had never before heard Ms. R use profanity.] This is my house, you have no right to be here.' I felt good on waking up. In the dream I wasn't frightened of the people who had taken over my house, I was irate."

I said, "The house is the place in which you live, a place that is yours and yours alone." Ms. R and I talked about the way in which the dream reflected her growing capacity to firmly lay claim to a place in which to live that is entirely hers, a place where she need not choose between killing herself or killing someone else who is occupying her. "In the dream, the people who had moved into my house were not going to die if I sent them away. They would simply have to find another place to live."

Ms. R had been living in a psychotic world generated by and with her mother (with the help of her father), a world in which the patient was, at every moment, unconsciously feeling that she had to choose between killing herself (giving herself over to being a projection of her mother's feelings of her own vileness) or killing her mother by insisting on becoming a person in her own right (albeit a person who had no real mother and no world that held meaning for her).

The thinking that I consider transformative thinking in my work with Ms. R was the thinking that the patient and I did together in the course of years of analysis—thinking that eventually led to a radical transformation in the way the patient and I ordered experience, creating a gestalt that transcended the terms of the emotional world in which she and I had lived. Ms. R, in this newly created way of generating and ordering experience, was able to feel feelings such as kindness, love, tenderness, sadness, and remorse, which up to that point had been only words that others used to refer to feelings she had never been able to feel. The intimacy and affection that Ms. R and I were now capable of feeling were alive for both of us when she spoke of a world in which "you and I talk like this." Even Ms. R's use of the words "you and I" in this phrase, as opposed to "we," conveyed a feeling of loving separateness, as opposed to engulfing, annihilating union. So simple a difference in use of language is communicative of the radical transformation in the patient's thinking and being.

The fundamentally new emotional terms that were created did not derive from self-hatred and pathological mutual dependence, but from Ms. R's wish and need to become a person in her own right, a person who was able to give and receive a form of love that she never before knew existed. It is a love that paradoxically takes pleasure in, and derives strength from, the separateness of the other person. Separateness in this new set of emotional terms, this new way of being alive, does not give rise to tyrannical efforts to incorporate or be incorporated by the other person; rather, it generates a genuine appreciation of the surprise, joy, sadness, and manageable fear that derive from the firm knowledge of one's own and the other person's independence.

While I believe that transformative thinking in this clinical account was a product of the entirety of the work with Ms. R, I also think that there were junctures in the work during which I sensed that Ms. R and I were engaged in something different from "ordinary" dream thinking. For example, as I have described, such a moment occurred in a session as I spoke to the patient about her hopelessness regarding the possibility of ever freeing herself of the need to make an impossible choice: whom to kill, herself or her mother? Though I could feel that a significant (and welcome) shift was occurring at that point, I was not able to attach words to, or even be clear with myself about, what I was feeling. As the session proceeded—a session in which a good deal of psychological work was done—the patient (unconsciously) helped me realize that I had come to experience her tenderly and sadly as the daughter I never had, and never would have. Paradoxically, in the very act of becoming aware of that emotional void in myself, I was experiencing with Ms. R feelings of father-daughter love and loss (separation) that constituted, for me (and I believe for Ms. R), a new way of being with oneself and with another person.

This transformative thinking was inseparable from another level of transformative thinking in which the patient and I were engaged during this session: Ms. R's coming to feel and understand at a profound psychological depth her self-imprisonment in a world cast almost exclusively in terms of the dilemma that becoming a person separate from her mother required either murder or suicide. The patient was able to begin to experience a way of being that was cast in radically different terms. She began to experience separation (becoming a person in her own right) not as an act of murder, but as an act of creating a place in herself (and between herself and me)—a place in which she was able to experience a previously inconceivable sense of who she was and who she was becoming.

Concluding comments

The shift of emphasis in contemporary psychoanalysis from an emphasis on *what* the patient thinks to *the way* he thinks has, I believe, significantly altered how we, as analysts, approach our clinical work. I have discussed three forms of thinking that figure prominently in the portions of the two analyses I have discussed. The first of these forms of thinking—magical thinking—is thinking in name only; instead of generating genuine psychic change, it subverts thinking and psychological growth by substituting invented reality for disturbing external reality. The omnipotent fantasying that underlies magical thinking is solipsistic in nature and contributes not only to preserving the current structure of the unconscious internal object world, but also to limiting the possibility of learning from one's experience with real external objects.

By contrast, dream thinking is our most profound form of thinking. It involves viewing and processing experience from a multiplicity of vantage points simultaneously, including the perspective of primary and secondary process thinking; of the container and the contained; of the paranoid-schizoid, depressive, and autistic-contiguous positions;

of the magical and the real; of the infantile self and the mature self; and so on. Unlike magical thinking, dream thinking "works" in the sense that it facilitates genuine psychological growth. While dream thinking may be generated by an individual on his own, there is always a point beyond which it requires two (or more) people to think/ dream one's most disturbing emotional experience.

Transformative thinking is a form of dream thinking in which one achieves a radical psychological shift—a psychological movement from one's current conceptual/experiential gestalt to a new, previously unimaginable ordering of experience. Such movement creates the potential for generating types of feeling, forms of object relatedness, and qualities of aliveness that the individual has never before experienced. This sort of thinking always requires the minds of at least two people, since an individual in isolation from others cannot radically alter the fundamental categories of meaning by which he orders his experience.

References

Barros, E. M. and Barros, E. L. (2008). Reflections on the clinical implications of symbolism in dream life. Presented to the Brazilian Psychoanalytic Society of Saõ Paulo, August.

Bion, W. R. (1957). Differentiation of the psychotic and non-psychotic personalities. In *Second thoughts* (pp. 43–64). New York: Aronson, 1967.

Bion, W. R. (1959). *Experiences in groups and other papers*. New York: Basic Books.

Bion, W. R. (1962a). Learning from experience. In *Seven servants*. New York: Aronson, 1977.

Bion, W. R. (1962b). A theory of thinking. In *Second thoughts* (pp. 110–119). New York: Aronson, 1967.

Bion, W. R. (1965). Transformations. In *Seven servants*. New York: Aronson, 1977.

Bion, W. R. (1970). Attention and interpretation. In *Seven servants*. New York: Aronson, 1977.

Bion, W. R. (1987). Clinical seminars. In F. Bion ed., *Clinical seminars and other works* (pp. 1–240). London: Karnac.

de M'Uzan, M. (1984). Les enclaves de la quantité. *Nouvelle Revue de Psychanalyse*, 30, 129–138.

de M'Uzan, M. (2003). Slaves of quantity. *Psychoanalytic Quarterly*, 72, 711–725.

Fairbairn, W. R. D. (1944). Endopsychic structure considered in terms of object-relationships. In *Psychoanalytic studies of the personality* (pp. 82–136). London: Routledge/Kegan Paul, 1952.

Ferro, A. (1999). *The bi-personal field: Experiences in child analysis*. London: Routledge.

Freud, S. (1900). The interpretation of dreams. *S. E.*, 4/5.

Freud, S. (1909). Notes upon a case of obsessional neurosis. *S. E.*, 10.

Freud, S. (1911). Formulations on the two principles of mental functioning. *S. E.*, 12.

Freud, S. (1913). Totem and taboo. *S. E.*, 13.

Freud, S. (1923). The ego and the id. *S. E.*, 19.

Freud, S. (1926). Inhibitions, symptoms and anxiety. *S. E.*, 20.

Freud, S. (1933). New introductory lectures on psycho-analysis. *S. E.*, 22.

Gaddini, E. (1969). On imitation. *International Journal of Psychoanalysis*, 50, 475–484.

Grotstein, J. S. (2000). *Who is the dreamer who dreams the dream? A study of psychic presences*. Hillsdale, NJ: Analytic Press.

Grotstein, J. S. (2009). Dreaming as a "curtain of illusion": Revisiting the "royal road" with Bion as our guide. *International Journal of Psychoanalysis*, 90, 733–752.

Heaney, S. (1986). The government of the tongue. In *The government of the tongue: Selected prose, 1978–1987* (pp. 91–108). New York: Farrar, Straus and Giroux, 1988.

Klein, M. (1935). A contribution to the psychogenesis of manic-depressive states. In *Contributions to psycho-analysis, 1921–1945* (pp. 282–310). London: Hogarth, 1968.

Klein, M. (1946). Notes on some schizoid mechanisms. In *Envy and gratitude and other works, 1946–1963* (pp. 1–24). New York: Delacorte Press/ Seymour Lawrence, 1975.

Klein, M. (1948). On the theory of anxiety and guilt. In *Envy and gratitude and other works, 1946–1963* (pp. 25–32). New York: Delacorte Press/ Seymour Lawrence, 1975.

Klein, M. (1952). The mutual influences in the development of ego and id. In *Envy and gratitude and other works, 1946–1963* (pp. 57–60). New York: Delacorte Press/Seymour Lawrence, 1975.

McDougall, J. (1984). The "dis-affected" patient: Reflections on affect pathology. *Psychoanalytic Quarterly*, 53, 386–409.

Ogden, T. H. (1989). On the concept of an autistic-contiguous position. *International Journal of Psychoanalysis*, 70, 127–140.

Ogden, T. H. (1994a). The analytic third: Working with intersubjective clinical facts. *International Journal of Psychoanalysis*, 75, 3–20.

Ogden, T. H. (1994b). *Subjects of analysis*. Northvale, NJ: Aronson; London: Karnac.

Ogden, T. H. (1997a). Reverie and interpretation. *Psychoanalytic Quarterly*, 66, 567–595.

Ogden, T. H. (1997b). *Reverie and interpretation: Sensing something human*. Northvale, NJ: Aronson; London: Karnac.

Ogden, T. H. (2004a). On holding and containing, being and dreaming. *International Journal of Psychoanalysis*, 85, 1349–1364.

Ogden, T. H. (2004b). This art of psychoanalysis: Dreaming undreamt dreams and interrupted cries. *International Journal of Psychoanalysis*, 85, 857–877.

Ogden, T. H. (2005). *This art of psychoanalysis: Dreaming undreamt dreams and interrupted cries*. London: Routledge.

Ogden, T. H. (2010). Why read Fairbairn? *International Journal of Psychoanalysis*, 91, 101–118.

Pontalis, J.-B. (2003). *Windows* (A. Quinney, Trans.). Lincoln, NB/London: University of Nebraska Press.

Rosenfeld, H. (1987). *Impasse and interpretation*. London: Tavistock.

Sandler, J. (1976). Dreams, unconscious fantasies and "identity of perception." *International Journal of Psychoanalysis*, 3, 33–42.

Tustin, F. (1981). *Autistic states in children*. Boston, MA: Routledge/Kegan Paul.

Winnicott, D. W. (1956). Primary maternal preoccupation. In *Through paediatrics to psycho-analysis* (pp. 300–305). New York: Basic Books, 1975.

Winnicott, D. W. (1971). *Playing and reality*. New York: Basic Books.

FEAR OF BREAKDOWN AND THE UNLIVED LIFE

There are a small handful of psychoanalytic papers and books that have most affected the ways I think, not simply about psychoanalysis, but about what it is to be alive as a human being. I would include in that group Freud's (1917) "Mourning and melancholia," Fairbairn's (1944) "Endopsychic structure considered in terms of object-relationships," Klein's (1946) "Notes on some schizoid mechanisms," Bion's (1962) *Learning from experience*, and Loewald's (1979) "The waning of the Oedipus complex," as well as the paper on which I focus in the present chapter, Winnicott's (1974) "Fear of breakdown."

Winnicott thinking aloud about fear of breakdown

"Fear of breakdown" (1974), written in the last year of Winnicott's life and published three years after his death, is to my mind, his last major work.[1] As in so many of his most important papers, this one

---

1 There is some uncertainty about when Winnicott wrote "Fear of breakdown." In an editorial note to the initial publication of this paper in the *International Review of Psychoanalysis*, Mrs. Clare Winnicott (1974) writes: "This particular paper was offered for posthumous publication because it was written shortly before Donald Winnicott's death [in 1971] and it contains a first condensed statement based on current clinical work. The formulation of these clinical findings around the central idea contained in the paper was a significant experience. Something surfaced from the depths of clinical involvement into conscious grasp and produced a new orientation to a whole area of clinical practice. It was the intention to study further

might be summarized in a sentence or two unless one takes the time to look closely at the complexity that lies beneath the deceptively simple surface. In reading the opening lines of the paper, there can be no doubt that Winnicott believed that he had come to understand something that was new to him and important for him to communicate before he died. The paper begins:

My clinical experiences have brought me recently to a new understanding, as I believe, of the meaning of fear of breakdown. (p. 87)

Unobtrusively, the word "experiences" is there in the opening phrase of the paper—such an ordinary word, and yet it lies at the very heart of the essay. The words "recently" and "new" in this sentence are followed by the use of the word "new" twice more in the next sentence:

It is my purpose here to state as simply as possible this which is new for me and which perhaps is new for others who work in psychotherapy. (p. 87)

He writes in the third and fourth sentences of the essay:

Naturally, if what I say has truth in it, this will already have been dealt with by the world's poets, but the flashes of insight that come in poetry cannot absolve us from our painful task of getting step by step away from ignorance toward our goal. It is my opinion that a study of this limited area leads to a restatement of several other problems that puzzle us as we fail to do as well clinically as we would wish to do. . . . (p. 87)

---

some of the specific topics in the paper, and to write about them in greater detail, but time did not allow this work to be done" (p. 103). In *Psychoanalytic explorations* (1989), a selection of Winnicott's published and unpublished papers, the editors, who include Clare Winnicott, date "Fear of breakdown" as "Written in 1963?" My own reading of the paper would lead me to believe that the sketch-like nature of this article, written on a subject very important to Winnicott, would support Clare Winnicott's (1974) statement that it was written close to the time of his death.

Who, other than Winnicott, could have written these words? And even Winnicott, so far as my memory serves me, has not previously written in quite this way. He tells us that if there is any truth in what he believes he has discovered and hopes to convey, it will no doubt be a truth that poets have known and captured in poetry. But we, as therapists, do not have the luxury of settling for flashes of insight. The poets' brief understandings do not "absolve us from our painful task of getting step by step away from ignorance toward our goal." The language is almost religious in tone. Our responsibility to our patients does not allow us to "absolve us from our painful task" of using ourselves in ways that we must if we are to be of help to our patients. To do this we must get "step by step away from ignorance." What sort of ignorance? Certainly not ignorance of analytic theory (a knowledge of which Winnicott twice states later in the paper he assumes the reader possesses). As I understand these words, the ignorance we must overcome is an emotional ignorance of ourselves. It is necessary that we be able to experience what is most painful in our lives and come to understand ourselves with regard to those experiences. The tone is not that of preaching, but of humility and remorse in the face of his own failures (only later in the paper do we learn of the suicide of one of Winnicott's patients).

Winnicott tells us that he believes that what he has learned about "this limited area" ("the meaning of a fear of breakdown") may help us arrive at understandings of other problems that contribute to our failing our patients. It is unmistakable when reading these lines that Winnicott fervently wishes to convey what he has learned while he is still able to do so.

Winnicott's writing throughout his analytic life is moving, not because he wears his heart on his sleeve. In fact, he says very little (directly) about his own inner life, much less the specifics of his life outside of the consulting room. His writing is moving because he is able to convey, through his use of language, what it is to be alive to the experiences he is describing and to the ideas that he is developing (which, as he says in the opening phrase of this paper, are inseparable from his experiences).

One could easily rush through "the preliminaries" that I have just quoted from the opening of "Fear of breakdown," eager to get on to the meat of the paper. But to do so would be to miss the essence of the paper: Winnicott in these initial sentences is *showing* the reader what it means to live (to be alive to) one's experience, both in his own act of writing and (potentially) in the reader's act of reading.

Winnicott says that what he will be addressing are "universal phenomena" (p. 88), though they may be more evident in some of our patients. Most important, these universal phenomena:

> indeed make it possible for everyone to know empathetically what it feels like when one of our patients shows this fear [of breakdown] in a big way. (The same can be said, indeed, of every detail of the insane person's insanity. We all know about it, although this particular detail [this aspect of insanity] may not be bothering us [at the moment].) (p. 87)

How could Winnicott make his point more clearly and forcefully: to be an adequate therapist we must make use of our own personal knowledge of "what it feels like"—what "insanity" feels like— even though we are not in the full grip of a particular "detail" of that insanity at a given moment.

As in "The use of an object" (1967),[2] Winnicott, in "Fear of breakdown," invents a new, purposefully disorienting language for what he is trying to convey. In "Fear of breakdown," Winnicott tears terms away from their ordinary usage in a way that succeeds in destabilizing the reader. Principal among these words made anew is the term *breakdown*:

> I have purposely used the term "breakdown" because it is rather vague and because it could mean various things. On the whole the word can be taken in this context to mean a failure of defence organization. But immediately we ask: a defence against what? And this leads us to the deeper meaning of the term, since we need to use the word "breakdown" to describe the unthinkable state of affairs that underlies the defence organisation. (1974, p. 88)

---

2 In "The use of an object," Winnicott uses the term *object-relating*, which ordinarily refers to mature object-relatedness, to refer to primitive relatedness in which the object is "a bundle of projections" (1967, p. 88); and he uses the term *object usage*, which usually connotes taking advantage of another person, to refer to a mature form of object relatedness in which one recognizes the other as a subject like oneself and grasps the fact that the other person lies beyond the reach of one's psychic omnipotence.

Each time I read this passage, my head begins to spin. A set of interrelated terms is introduced, the meanings of which slip and slide. I try to take it sentence by sentence. Winnicott says:

> On the whole the word [breakdown] can be taken in this context to mean a failure of a defence organisation. (p. 88)

So far so good: breakdown is the failure of a defense organization. The next sentence reads:

> But immediately we ask: a defence against what? (p. 88)

Winnicott offers an answer to this question:

> we need to use the term "breakdown" to describe the unthinkable state of affairs that underlies the defence organisation. (p. 88)

Here it gets confusing: Winnicott seems to be saying that "breakdown" (which he said only a sentence earlier was the failure of a defense organization) is also the unthinkable state of affairs "underlying" the defense organization. I wonder, "How can breakdown mean both the failure of the defense organization and the unthinkable that lies beneath that organization?"

As if this tangle of questions were not confusing enough, Winnicott adds in the succeeding paragraph: what "lies behind the defences" are "psychotic phenomena" that involve "a breakdown of the establishment of the unit self" (p. 88). (The unit self is "a state in which the infant is a unit, a whole person, with an inside and an outside, and a person living in a body, and more or less bounded by the skin" [Winnicott, 1963, p. 91]. "In achieving unit status . . . the infant becomes a person, an individual in his own right" [Winnicott, 1960, p. 44].)

So what do we have so far? A "breakdown" is the failure of a defense organization that was constructed to protect the individual from an unthinkable psychotic state of affairs that involves the "breakdown of the establishment of the unit self." One problem here lies in the fact that the word "breakdown" is being used in several different ways. Another problem lies in the fact that the word "breakdown" is being used repeatedly in the very effort to define the term "breakdown."

51

I believe that the confusing way the word *breakdown* is being defined is the product of the fact that Winnicott is thinking as he is writing, or to put it the other way round, he is using writing as a medium in which to think. As he said at the outset, all of this is new to him and, I would add, he is not quite sure how to put it into words. His words are not devoid of meaning; rather, the meaning is in the process of being thought out and more carefully defined.

Many questions have arisen:

- Is a breakdown a psychotic break, a breaking up of the mind (or of unit status)?
- Does the defense organization (which is itself psychotic in nature) serve to ward off an even worse psychotic catastrophe?
- Is psychosis the "unthinkable state of affairs" that "underlies the defence organization"?
- How does the breakdown become ensconced in the future in the form of a "fear of breakdown"?

The reader must be patient and tolerate confusion as Winnicott works out the problem of defining the nature of the "breakdown" that is the subject of his paper. As is so often the case in reading Winnicott, the effects he creates in his writing reflect qualities of the analytic experience he is discussing. As we shall see, these confusing effects that Winnicott creates in his discussion of "breakdown" convey something of the confusion inherent in a state of mind in which the past does not yet have a present, and the present does not yet have a past.

Lived and unlived experience

Winnicott then seems to make a fresh attempt at approaching the topic, which he begins by stating for himself the fundamental processes belonging to the early stages of emotional growth. He begins where we must all begin in reading Winnicott:

> The individual inherits a maturational process. This carries an individual along in so far as there exists a facilitating environment . . . the essential feature [of which] is that it has a kind of growth of its own, being adapted to the changing needs of the growing individual. (1974, p. 102)

With this statement of the early mother-infant relationship in mind, Winnicott offers a list of "primitive agonies" (p. 90)—a form of pain for which "anxiety is not a strong enough word" (p. 89)—each followed by the defense organization that is meant to protect against experiencing the underlying primitive agony "which is unthinkable" (p. 90). These agonies occur during a period when the individual is in a state of absolute dependence—a time when the mother is "supplying an auxiliary ego function . . . a time when the infant has not separated the 'not-me' from the 'me'" (p. 89). The primitive agonies and the ways we defend against them include:

1 A return to an unintegrated state. (Defence: disintegration.)
2 Falling forever. (Defence: self-holding.)
3 Loss of psychosomatic collusion, failure of indwelling. (Defence: depersonalization.)
4 Loss of sense of real. (Defence: exploitation of primary narcissism, etc.)
5 Loss of capacity to relate to objects. (Defence: autistic states, relating only to self-phenomena.)
   And so on. (pp. 89–90)

The reader must do a good deal of work here: he must not only read the paper, he must also write it. I view "Fear of breakdown" as something of an unfinished paper (in my opinion, written at the very end of Winnicott's life). In my reading of this paper, I do not try to figure out what Winnicott "really meant." Instead, I take Winnicott's explicitly and implicitly stated ideas as a starting point for the development of my own thinking.[3] I approach the primitive agonies listed above from the point of view that each of them, for instance, "A return to an unintegrated state," *is an agony only because it occurs in the absence of a good enough mother-infant bond* (a state of affairs that Winnicott calls a failure of the facilitating environment[4]). As Winnicott

---

3 A good deal has been written about "Fear of breakdown." It is beyond the scope of this paper to compare my own reading with those of others. Among the papers and books that discuss this work, a few stand out in my mind as having particular bearing on the aspects of the paper on which I am focusing: Abram (2012), Gaddini (1981), Green (2010), and C. Winnicott (1980).
4 It seems to me that Winnicott oversimplifies the concept of breakdown in this paper when he attributes its source to "a failure of the facilitating environment."

(1971) makes clear in "Basis for self in body," the infant may "at times disintegrate, depersonalize and even for a moment abandon the almost fundamental urge to exist and to feel existent" (p. 261). The capacity to move among these states is a healthy condition when experienced *within the context of a healthy mother-infant tie.*

The infant who is in an unintegrated state, *by himself*—outside of the mother-infant tie—is in a terrifying state. To protect himself, Winnicott suggests, the infant makes use of the psychotic defense of disintegration, that is, he preemptively annihilates himself ("defence: disintegration"). The central point here, I believe—though I must read it into the paper—is that feeling states that are tolerable in the context of the mother-infant bond are primitive agonies when the infant must experience them on his own. I "write" into Winnicott's stark list of agonies and their defenses the following: When disconnected from the mother, the infant, instead of experiencing the agony, short-circuits the experience and substitutes for it a psychotic defense organization (such as disintegration).

Similarly, the primitive agony that Winnicott calls "falling forever" is short-circuited (not experienced) because it would be unbearable for the infant to experience it *by himself.* I imagine that the agony of falling forever is an experience like that depicted in Kubrick's (1968) film *2001: A space odyssey,* in which an astronaut floats alone into endless, silent, empty space after the umbilical cord to the spacecraft is severed.

In order not to experience the unbearable agony of falling forever, the infant defends himself by means of "self-holding"—a desperate attempt, in the absence of the mother, to hold his very being together. Again, the pivotal idea here is *that the feeling of falling forever is only an agony when the infantile self is disconnected from the mother* (a point left to the reader to write).

Winnicott, still preparing for what he calls his "Statement of Main Theme," says:

It seems odd that Winnicott, always the pediatrician, does not acknowledge the myriad contributions to breaches in, as opposed to failures of, the facilitating environment, such as hypersensitivity on the part of the infant that makes the infant inconsolable regardless of how good the mothering (the facilitating environment) may be, an infant's severe and/or chronic physical illness; and so on.

It is wrong to think of psychotic illness as a breakdown, it is a defence organisation relative to primitive agony. (1974, p. 90)

So one of the questions left unanswered in the early part of the paper is addressed: the term "breakdown," as Winnicott is using it, is not synonymous with psychotic break; rather, the psychosis resides in the defensive organization that the individual uses to protect himself from the experience of "primitive agony." Still left unaddressed, however, is the question: If "breakdown" is not a psychotic break, what is it?

Only at this point in the paper is Winnicott ready for what he calls "Statement of Main Theme," in which he addresses the question: What does he mean by breakdown? He begins to explain: "I contend that clinical fear of breakdown is *the fear of a breakdown that has already been experienced*" (p. 90). It seems to me that for some reason Winnicott has mis-stated his main theme. What I think he means, and what he later says several times, is that the fear of breakdown is a fear of a breakdown that has *already happened*, but has *not yet been experienced*. In other words, we have ways of experiencing or not experiencing the events of our lives.

Winnicott's thinking about the relationship of past to present in a breakdown that occurs, but is not experienced, differs from Freud's (1918) concept of "deferred action" (*Nachträglichkeit*). The latter refers to the way "experiences, impressions and memory traces may be revised at a later date to fit in with fresh experiences or with the attainment of a new stage of development" (Laplanche and Pontalis, 1973, p. 111). In deferred action, the event *has been experienced*, but its meaning changes with the individual's psychological development. In fear of breakdown, the event has not been experienced, and it is this attribute that defines its relationship with the present.[5]

---

5 Faimberg (2007, 2013) makes an important contribution to the discussion of the relationship between past and present in "Fear of breakdown" (and in *Nachträglichkeit* in general). She conceives of the experiencing of a past event *for the first time* in the present as involving a "*twofold* movement: one of anticipation (primitive agony) and another of retrospection (given by the analyst's words)" (2013, p. 208). It seems to me that Faimberg's idea of "anticipation" and "retrospection" engaged in a "*twofold* movement" conveys the sense of a not-yet-experienced past "seeking" an experiential state in the present, and at the same time, the present "seeking" in the past what is lacking in its current state.

I believe that closer to Winnicott's conception of an event that is not experienced is the work of the French Psychosomatic School, for whom emotional experience that is too disturbing for the individual to bear is foreclosed from psychical elaboration and relegated to the realm of the body, where somatic illness or perversion may develop (de M'Uzan, 1984; McDougall, 1984).

Winnicott, in taking up his "main theme," focuses first on the difficulty of working with patients who are in pain because they are not able to experience the breakdown that has occurred in the past, and instead suffer from fear of breakdown in the future:

> We cannot hurry up our patients. Nevertheless, we can hold up their progress because of genuinely not knowing; any little piece of our understanding may help us to keep up with a patient's needs. (1974, p. 90)

I think that what Winnicott is referring to when he says "any little piece of our understanding may help us to keep up with a patient's needs" is: we must be able to know (to *experience* our own) breakdown and primitive agony if we are to help the patient develop the capacity to experience his own breakdown and primitive agony.

Winnicott continues:

> There are moments, according to my experience, when a patient needs to be told that the breakdown, a fear of which destroys his or her life, *has already been.* It is a fact that is carried round hidden in the unconscious. (p. 90)

The breakdown occurred very early in the patient's life, but it was not experienced then. The fact of the early breakdown is "carried round hidden in the unconscious"; but the unconscious, he explains, is not the unconscious of Freud's repressed unconscious, nor is it the unconscious of Freud's instinct-driven id, nor is it the Jungian archetypal unconscious. Winnicott states:

> In this special context [of a breakdown that has already occurred, but has not been experienced] *the unconscious means that the ego integration is not able to encompass something.*" (pp. 90–91, emphasis added)

In this sentence, I believe that Winnicott is proposing an extension of the analytic conception of the unconscious. The unconscious, in addition to constituting a psychic domain for experiencing the repressed aspects of life that have occurred and *have been experienced*, but are so disturbing as to be banned from conscious awareness, also involves an aspect of the individual (often more physical than psychical) where there exist registrations of events that have occurred, but *have not been experienced*. The latter is the aspect of the individual that carries his unassimilated traumatic experience, his "undreamt dreams" (Ogden, 2004b).

Now it is possible to respond to other questions raised, but not answered, earlier in this paper: What does Winnicott mean by "breakdown"? Is breakdown the breaking down of the mind in psychosis? Is the "defensive organisation" a defense against psychosis, a defense against breakdown, or a defense against primitive agony? Again, what I am about to say is my own reading/writing of Winnicott's paper. To my mind, the term "breakdown" refers to the breakdown of the mother-infant tie, which leaves the infant alone and raw and on the verge of not existing. The infant in this state—disconnected from the mother—is thrust into what might become an experience of primitive agony. But the experiencing of the primitive agony does not occur (or is short-circuited) because the infant, whose very being is threatened, makes use, in a thorough-going way, of a defense organization that shuts out the experience of primitive agony. So, it seems to me, that the term *breakdown* refers to the break in the mother-infant tie, not to a psychotic break. The psychosis lies in the *defense* against the experience of the break in the mother-infant tie.

Winnicott elaborates in the subsequent sentence:

The ego [of an infant or child who has experienced breakdown] is too immature to gather all the phenomena into the area of personal omnipotence. (1974, p. 91)

In reading this paper, I am always stopped dead in my tracks here. What does it mean to not be able "to gather all the phenomena into the area of personal omnipotence"? What is the area of personal omnipotence? Is this form of omnipotence "personal" because the individual is sufficiently mature to be able to engage in this way of thinking on his own? Winnicott makes it clear that he views this type of thinking (in the "area of personal omnipotence") as a part of healthy development.

What follows is my own interpretation of Winnicott's statement concerning the inability of the immature ego to gather phenomena

57

into the area of personal omnipotence. I think that the term "personal omnipotence" refers to the background feeling state of the internal world of a person who has achieved unit status, someone who has become a person in his own right. If this supposition is accurate, omnipotence, in this context, refers to an internalization of early experience with a mother who was able to create for the infant the illusion that the world is just as he wants it and needs it to be. Although the mother (the facilitating environment) matures in a way that is responsive to the infant's growing need for "negative care and alive neglect" (Winnicott, 1949, p. 245), which facilitates the infant's development toward unit status, the early experience of "omnipotence"—the experience of the world being just as it should be—remains an element of the healthy, unconscious internal world of the individual.

With this conception of the unconscious in mind, Winnicott goes on to address another of the questions raised at the outset of the paper: How does the breakdown become ensconced in the future in the form of a "fear of breakdown"? Winnicott's response to this question constitutes what I find to be one of the most beautifully written passages in his paper:

> It must be asked here: why does the patient go on being worried [fearing what will happen in the future] by this that belongs to the past? The answer must be that the original experience of primitive agony cannot get into the past unless the ego can first gather it into its own present time experience and into omnipotent control now (assuming the auxiliary ego-supporting function of the mother (analyst)).
>
> In other words, the patient *must go on looking* for the past detail which is not yet experienced. The search takes the form of a looking for this detail in the future. (1974, p. 91, emphasis added)

So, the past event that occurred, but was not experienced, continues to torment the patient until it is lived in the present (with the mother/analyst). And yet, despite the beauty of Winnicott's response to the question he poses, I find his answer incomplete. It seems to me that *a principal, if not* the *principal motivation for an individual who has not experienced important parts of what happened in his early life is the urgent need to lay claim to those lost parts of himself, to finally complete himself by encompassing within himself as much of his unlived (unexperienced) life as he is able.* I view this as a universal need—the need on the part of every person to reclaim, or claim for the first time, what he has

lost of himself and, in so doing, take the opportunity to become the
person he still holds the potential to be. One does so despite the fact
that attempting to realize that potential to become more fully oneself
involves experiencing the pain (of breakdown and the primitive agony
that results from breakdown) that had been too much to bear in
infancy and childhood, and that has led to the loss of important aspects
of self.

There are two critical differences between experiencing these
events when they happened in infancy and experiencing them as
a patient in analysis: the patient is an adult now, not an infant or
child, and consequently has, to some extent, a more mature self-organ-
ization; and even more important, the patient is not alone when he
is with an analyst who is able to bear the patient's, and his own,
experiences of breakdown and of primitive agony.

It seems to me that we all, to different degrees, have had events
in our early lives that involved significant breakdowns in the mother-
infant tie to which we have responded with psychotic defense
organizations. Each of us is painfully aware that regardless of how
psychologically healthy we may appear to others (and at times to
ourselves), there are important ways in which we are not capable of
being alive to our experience, whether that be the experience of joy,
or the ability to love one or all of our children, or the capacity to
be generous to the point of giving up something highly important
to us, or the capacity to forgive someone (including ourselves) who
has done something that has hurt us profoundly, or of simply feeling
alive to the world around us and within us. These are but a few of
the myriad forms of emotional limitation that derive from having been
unable to live the breakdowns that occurred when we were infants
and children. Each of these limitations is an aspect of our unlived
life, what we have been, and continue to be, unable to experience.
We all have our own particular areas of experience that we have
been unable to live, and we live in search of those lost potential
experiences, those lost parts of ourselves.

A good deal of analysis might be thought of as centrally involving
the analyst helping the patient to live his unlived life in the
transference–countertransference. Winnicott describes how the analyst
might facilitate the patient's ability to experience what I am calling
the unlived aspects of his life:

> [I]f the patient is ready for some kind of acceptance of this queer kind
> of truth, that what is not yet experienced did nevertheless happen in

59

the past, then the way is open for the agony to be experienced in the transference, in reaction to the analyst's failures and mistakes. These latter can be dealt with in doses that are not excessive, and the patient can account for each technical failure of the analyst as countertransference. In other words, gradually the patient gathers the original failure of the facilitating environment into the area of his or her omnipotence and the experience of omnipotence which belongs to the state of dependence (transference fact). (p. 91)

Here Winnicott presents in a few words his conception of how analysis works: in order for the experience of breakdown to get into the past tense, the individual must live the experience of what happened (then) in the transference (now). The way this happens in analysis is by means of patient and analyst living an experience together over time, an experience of failure on the part of the analyst that is significant, but not more than the patient can tolerate. Winnicott is clear that the analyst attempts to keep the experience of breakdown contained in the consulting room so that hospitalization is not necessary. Also, the experience of breakdown "is not good enough if it does not include analytic understanding and insight on the part of the patient" (p. 92). Winnicott does not envision a cure by catharsis. Psychological growth occurs by means of experience in, and understanding of, a lived analytic experience of failure of the mother/analyst in a situation of total dependence. Paradoxically, the analyst must simultaneously *fail* the patient in a significant way that breaks the tie between patient and analyst during a period of dependence, and *not fail* the patient by living the experience of the current breakdown with the patient and helping the patient to understand his experience of the breakdown.

Clinical illustrations

Winnicott offers only four brief clinical accounts in "Fear of breakdown." In one of these, a discussion of emptiness (pp. 93–95), he describes his work with a patient who did not experience a fear of emptiness or a fear of breakdown, and instead "supplied experience of an indirect kind" (p. 94). The state of mind that Winnicott views as underlying yet-to-be-experienced emptiness is merely a sense that "something might have been" (p. 94).

In the two clinical examples that I will offer, my focus, like Winnicott's in his discussion of emptiness, will not be on the ways in which fear of breakdown manifests itself as a projection into the future of a breakdown that occurred in the past. Instead, I will be focusing on the ways in which breakdown of the mother-infant tie in infancy and childhood generates unlived portions of an individual's life that become a continuous presence in the form of a sense of incompleteness of the self (analogous to Winnicott's idea that yet-to-be-experienced emptiness manifests itself in the present as a sense that "something might have been" [p. 94]).

In the present chapter, beginning in my discussion of theory, and now in the presentation of clinical material, I hope to convey the ways in which I conceive of, and work with, the patient's fundamental need to capture lost parts of himself or herself which have never come to life, have remained unlived (and thus persist only as a potential aspect of self). As I will illustrate, fundamental to helping a patient experience aspects of himself that have been "lost" (i.e., unrealized) is an analytic attitude that recognizes and values the most subtle and unlikely ways in which a patient may attempt to experience for the first time unlived events of the past.

The first clinical experience that I will discuss occurred in a four-sessions-per-week analysis with a woman who had suffered from severe neglect as a child. Her mother was depressed—often unable to get out of bed—and her father deserted the family when the patient was two years old.

During this long analysis, Ms. L would repeatedly "fall in love" with men who seemed to her to return her love, but very soon acted as if they had never expressed any interest in her at all. After Ms. L had spent some time shopping for a car, she told me that a salesman at one of the dealerships had been very affectionate in the way he spoke to her. When they took a test drive, he talked about how much fun it would be to drive the car on the road that runs along Big Sur.

After buying the car, Ms. L returned to the dealership to see the salesman. She felt "crushed" when time and again, after talking with her for a few minutes, he "dropped" her to talk "with just anybody" who walked through the front door of the showroom. After being "ignored" by him during that visit, the patient felt "devastated by his duplicity." For the subsequent two weeks, Ms. L each day parked her car across the street from the dealership to watch the salesman. During the months that followed, the patient could think of little other than how much she longed for this man.

I spoke with Ms. L about the possible connection between her disappointing, maddening, humiliating experience with the salesman and her feeling that I, too, drop her repeatedly at the end of each session, during the weekends, and when I am away on vacation breaks. Ms. L, infuriated by such a suggestion, accused me of not believing that the man she was "involved with" had shown genuine interest in her. I did not challenge her belief or persist in commenting on the transference.

Even as I was talking with Ms. L about the similarities between the way she felt about the salesman and the way she felt about me, I experienced my comments as stereotypic and formulaic. It seemed to me that Ms. L had every right to object to them—the comments were impersonal, "off the rack," not made uniquely for her and what was going on between the two of us consciously and unconsciously. With Ms. L's help, I put a stop to the way I was talking to her.

I then attempted to let my mind "go loose" in order to attend to whatever thoughts and feelings occurred to me (my own reverie experience) during the sessions with Ms. L. But during the months subsequent to my thoughtless transference "interpretations," I became aware that my new tack also felt as if it was just another prefabricated "analytic technique." I could not will myself into freedom and aliveness of thought. I slowly came to the realization that what was most real about what was occurring between Ms. L and me was the experience of sterility on both our parts.

After many more months of living with this type of sterility in the analysis, I said to Ms. L, "You came to me originally because you felt humiliated by the way you get rejected by a man and then make it worse for yourself by what you call 'tracking' him. This may surprise you, but I've come to believe that whatever it is in you that makes you persist in tracking these men is the healthiest part of you."

Ms. L replied, "Are you making fun of me?"

I said, "No, I've never been more serious. You've told me that when you were a child you were left to raise yourself—your father left you, your mother withdrew from you. But your world of make-believe people was not an adequate substitute for a real childhood with real parents and real friends. I think that it's not an overstatement to say that you died when you were a small child for lack of affection and want of being seen for who you are. When you described watching the car salesman from across the street, it felt to me that you were like a dedicated detective who won't quit until she finds the missing person."

Ms. L said, "I've had the impression for some time now that you've given up on me, that you're continuing to meet with me only because you don't know how to get out of this."

I could not remember the last time that Ms. L had said anything that felt as honest and personal as this. I said, "That's why I told you that I thought that your tracking is the healthiest part of you. It's the part of you that hasn't given up on yourself, that refuses to give up on yourself before you've had a love relationship with a real person, a love that is genuinely returned as strongly as you give it."

Ms. L replied, "It's the part of me I feel most ashamed of. I feel pathetic when I'm sitting in my car watching a man, but I don't know what else to do."

I said, "I think that the tracking is what keeps you alive, it's a way of holding on tightly to a final thread connecting you to life. The alternative is to let yourself die, either literally or by living as a zombie."

Ms. L said, "I was terrified of zombies as a kid. I wasn't afraid of spiders or snakes or vampires or serial killers, but I was scared shitless of zombies."

This was the first time that Ms. L had used any obscenity, and the importance of her doing so now was not lost on either of us. It seemed to me to reflect a genuine loosening up of the patient's freedom to think and to speak her thoughts and feelings. In the very act of telling me how frightened she was of becoming one of the living dead, she was able to sling shit, so to speak, into the formerly sterile analytic field.

I said to Ms. L, "A person will die if you somehow remove the shit from his or her bowels. People need the bacteria that makes their shit smell so bad."

Ms. L's voice was much less constricted than usual as she said to me, "It's funny to hear you use the word 'shit.' I like it. It feels like we're school-aged kids breaking the rules and that you don't do that with anyone else but me. Strangely enough, I'm not feeling afraid of being expelled from analysis."

In the subsequent period of work with Ms. L, the liveliness of the session I have just described remained a presence along with bouts of intense fear, on Ms. L's part, that I was manipulating her. She said she was afraid that I was playing an "analytic game" with her in which I was duping her into taking seriously what happens between us while I look on, unmoved, from the outside. Her accusations were wounding to me to a degree, and in a way, that was unusual for me. I was fond of Ms. L and felt that I had been as honest with myself and with her (in my role as her analyst) as I was able to be.

I said to Ms. L, "I think that when you accuse me of being manipulative with you, you're showing me what it feels like not to be seen, to be invisible. You know far more than you want to about what it feels like to be invisible to the point that you don't exist, even to yourself."

Ms. L was silent for the remainder of that session in a way that felt profoundly sad to me.

As I look back now on this period of work with Ms. L, it seems to me that we persisted through a very long period of emotional sterility. During these years, one or the other of us would try to evade recognizing the state of affairs that existed between us (for example, in the form of my attempts to imitate an analytic experience with "prepackaged" transference interpretations and reverie experiences). We pressed on despite the sterility (her absence as a living, breathing, shitting human being), perhaps because we somehow knew that we had to experience it together before anything else could occur. The truth of the idea that she had died when she was very young could only have felt real to her after experiencing *with me* the lifelessness of the analysis—and feeling powerless to do anything about it. Only then were we able to find words—although it felt like the words, such as the word "shit," found us—to express what we were experiencing in the present moment.

In thinking about this clinical experience, one might ask how my understanding of what occurred in Ms. L's analysis differs from the ways I have found some of Fairbairn's (1944) ideas to be useful in my own clinical work (Ogden, 2010). I have had experiences with patients that I have understood in terms of addictive attachments between unconscious internal objects—for example, between Fairbairn's "libidinal ego" and "exciting object," and between "the internal saboteur" and "the rejecting object." I would say that there is a critical difference between Fairbairn's conception of addictive internal object relationships and the way I conceive of Ms. L's compulsive "tracking" behavior. Fairbairn's internal object world is constructed as an internalized version of *lived experiences* in unsatis-factory object relationships with the mother. By contrast, Ms. L's unconscious world was shaped primarily by *unlived experience* in unsatisfactory early object relationships with her mother. Ms. L's fierce determination to claim her unlived life was the motor that drove her symptomatic (tracking) activity. In that tracking behavior, Ms. L unwaveringly sought out the unlived, unexperienced aspects of herself and her life, past and present.

It seems to me that patients who experience the most extreme forms of fear of breakdown, such as Ms. L, feel oppressed by the fact that they have been unable to live (have been unable to be alive to) most of their life experience. Such patients find it excruciatingly painful to feel alive—even to the extent of feeling pleasure in response to the sensation of the soft warmth of the sun on their skin—because it stirs the pain of recognition of how much of their life has been unlived. They often feel bitter about the fact that life has been taken from them that they will never get back. That pain, I find, usually takes the form of a combination of physical pain (often as a part of actual physical illness) and emotional pain.

Since a good deal of the pain of unlived experience is stored in the body in what Bion (1948–1951) called a "protomental state" (p. 154), it is not surprising that my unconscious understanding of that pain very often takes the form of my own bodily experience while working with a patient. For a period of time while working with one such patient, Ms. Z, I experienced gnawing physical hunger during her sessions, which abated when I met with my next patient. It took quite a while for me to understand the way in which Ms. Z used me (took me in) as a substitute for her own unlived life.

Early in the analysis, Ms. Z told me that when she was asked by a neighbor whether she liked a certain restaurant in the neighborhood, she told the person that she had never been there, when in fact she had eaten there many times. As I look back on it, Ms. Z, in telling me this story, was saying more of the truth than either of us knew at the time: she had frequented the restaurant, but had never really been there, in the sense of having been alive to her experience of being there.

She told me years later that during those first years of the analysis, she had made a journal entry after each of the five sessions we had each week, but recorded only what I said, not a single word of her own. I understood Ms. Z's absence from her journal of the analysis as her way of recording her own non-existence, her own breakdown in the form of having broken from life.

The analysis was very difficult and I was never confident that I was helping Ms. Z to come alive to her experience. After many years of analytic work, I brought up the subject of ending the analysis. I said to the patient that it seemed to me that I had ceased being of help to her in making changes in the way she lived her life and that she might benefit from working with someone else.

Ms. Z responded by saying, "It never occurred to me that we would end this analysis before one or the other of us died." I thought, but did not say, that both of us were, in many respects, already dead. She continued: "In fact, I never thought of the analysis as being connected with change." For Ms. Z, change was a concept that held no meaning. The dead do not change, and she was dead. We would not end until one of us died physically (we both had already died mentally in the analysis).

It came as a surprise to me that my bringing up the idea of ending the analysis would serve as a powerful impetus for a discussion of the patient's deadness, my deadness with her, and the deadness of the analysis. Ms. Z said in the session following the one in which I brought up ending the analysis that there were some things she wanted to accomplish in her life before we ended: she wanted to get married, complete her research, and publish that research as a book. In the course of the subsequent years of analysis, Ms. Z did accomplish all of these goals. She and I discussed the fact that getting married is different from making a marriage, and that there was a great deal of work ahead of her after we stopped, if she was to achieve that goal. We ended the analysis five years after I first broached the topic.

In the years since we stopped working together, Ms. Z has written to me about twice a year. In those letters she has told me that she feels that the end of the analysis was not an arbitrary thing; it now makes sense to her that we ended when we did and how we did. It was imperative that she live a life of her own, not one borrowed or stolen from me. Her life now feels like her own to do with what she can, and she feels grateful to me for waking her up to that fact before "I wrote off the entirety of my life."

I believe that Ms. Z did not consciously experience a fear of death because she was, in an important sense, already dead. For Ms. Z, being dead, being absent from her own life, was a way of protecting herself both from the pain of experiencing in the present a yet-to-be-lived past, as well as the pain of realizing that she was "missing" (in both senses of the word) important parts of herself.

Summary

Winnicott's "Fear of breakdown" is both an ending, in the sense of being his last major paper, and a beginning, in the sense that the paper introduces a new line of thought to be developed by others. It is a difficult essay, often confusing and opaque. It requires that the reader be not only a reader, but also a writer of this work that often gestures toward meaning as opposed to presenting fully developed ideas. My own interpretation of "Fear of breakdown" begins with the idea that the breakdown on which Winnicott is focusing is a breakdown in the mother-infant bond. Unable to bear, *on his own*, the primitive agonies that result from the break in the bond with the mother, the infant short-circuits the event in such a way that he does not experience it, and substitutes for it defenses of a psychotic nature. By not experiencing the breakdown when it occurred in infancy, the individual creates a psychological state in which he lives in fear of a breakdown that has already happened, but which he did not experience. I suggest that the driving force of the individual's need to find the source of his fear is his feeling that a part of his life has been taken from him, and what has been left for him is a life that is, in important ways, an unlived life.

References

Abram, J. (2012). On Winnicott's clinical innovations in the analysis of adults. *International Journal of Psychoanalysis*, 93, 1461–1473.

Bion, W. R. (1948–1951). Experiences in groups. In *Experiences in groups and other papers* (pp. 29–141). New York: Basic Books, 1959.

Bion, W. R. (1962). *Learning from experience*. New York: Basic Books.

de M'Uzan, M. (1984). Slaves of quantity. *Psychoanalytic Quarterly*, 72, 711–725.

Faimberg, H. (2007). A plea for a broader concept of *Nachträglichkeit*. *Psychoanalytic Quarterly*, 76, 1221–1240.

Faimberg, H. (1998/2013). *Nachträglichkeit* and Winnicott's "Fear of breakdown." In J. Abram (ed.), *Donald Winnicott today* (pp. 205–212). London: Routledge, 2013.

Fairbairn, W. R. D. (1944). Endopsychic structure considered in terms of object-relationships. In *Psychoanalytic studies of the personality* (pp. 82–136). London: Routledge/Kegan Paul, 1952.

Freud, S. (1917). Mourning and melancholia. *S. E.*, 14 (pp. 242–258).

Freud, S. (1918). From the history of an infantile neurosis. *S. E.*, 17 (pp. 7–121).

Gaddini, R. (1981). Bion's 'catastrophic change' and Winnicott's 'breakdown.' *Rivista di Psicoanalisi*, 27, 610–621.

Green, A. (2010). Sources and vicissitudes of being in D. W. Winnicott's work. *Psychoanalytic Quarterly*, 79, 11–36.

Klein, M. (1946). Notes on some schizoid mechanisms. In *Envy and gratitude and other works, 1946–1963* (pp. 1–24). New York: Delacorte Press/Seymour Laurence, 1975.

Kubrick, S. (dir). (1968). *2001: A space odyssey*. Metro-Goldwyn-Mayer.

Laplanche, J. and Pontalis, J.-B. (1973). *The language of psycho-analysis* (D. Nicholson-Smith, Trans.). New York: Norton.

Loewald, H. (1979). The waning of the Oedipus complex. In *Papers on psychoanalysis* (pp. 384–404). New Haven, CT: Yale University Press, 1980.

McDougall, J. (1984). The "dis-affected" patient: Reflections on affect pathology. *Psychoanalytic Quarterly*, 53, 386–409.

Ogden, T. H. (2004). This art of psychoanalysis: Dreaming undreamt dreams and interrupted cries. *International Journal of Psychoanalysis*, 85, 857–877.

Ogden, T. H. (2010). Why read Fairbairn? *International Journal of Psychoanalysis*, 91, 101–118.

Winnicott, C. (1974). Editorial note. Fear of breakdown, D. W. Winnicott. *International Review of Psychoanalysis*, 1, 102.

Winnicott, C. (1980). Fear of breakdown: A clinical example. *International Review of Psychoanalysis*, 61, 351–357.

Winnicott, D. W. (1949). Mind and its relation to the psyche-soma. In *Through paediatrics to psycho-analysis* (pp. 243–254). New York: Basic Books, 1958.

Winnicott, D. W. (1960). The theory of the parent–infant relationship. In *The maturational processes and the facilitating environment* (pp. 33–55). New York: International Universities Press, 1965.

Winnicott, D. W. (1963). From dependence towards independence in the development of the individual. In *The maturational processes and the facilitating environment* (pp. 83–92). New York: International Universities Press, 1965.

Winnicott, D. W. (1967). The use of an object and relating through identifications. In *Playing and reality* (pp. 86–94). New York: Basic Books, 1971.

Winnicott, D. W. (1971). Basis for self in body. In C. Winnicott, R. Shepherd, and M. Davis (eds), *Psychoanalytic explorations* (pp. 261–271). Cambridge, MA: Harvard University Press, 1989.

Winnicott, D. W. ([1971]1974). Fear of breakdown. In C. Winnicott, R. Shepherd, and M. Davis (eds), *Psychoanalytic explorations* (pp. 87–95). Cambridge, MA: Harvard University Press, 1989.

4

INTUITING THE TRUTH OF
WHAT'S HAPPENING

On Bion's "Notes on memory
and desire"

An individual's ideas are only as valuable as the use to which they are put by others. It has taken me thirty years of studying Bion's "Notes on memory and desire" (1967a) to be able to put into words something of what I have made with this paper. It is an impossibly difficult paper, and I have long ago accepted the fact that I will never understand it. It is only recently that I have recognized that my effort to understand the paper is misplaced. It is a paper that asks not to be understood. It asks of the reader something more difficult than understanding, and promises the reader something more valuable than understanding.

The paper, I now realize, is not about memory and desire; it is about intuitive thinking and the ways in which intuitive thinking works in the analytic situation; about the fact that we cannot be taught how to interpret what we sense concerning the patient's unconscious psychic truths. Nor can we be taught how to convey to the patient that we have intuited those truths, much less what it is that we have intuited; nor can we be taught whether it is wise to convey now, or perhaps tomorrow, something of what we sense about the patient's unconscious psychic reality, or whether it might be best never to convey what we sense concerning those truths that the patient holds most sacred.

So, when I ask myself what the chapter I am writing is about, I have to say that I am trying to write "Memory and desire" as my own paper, not in the sense of passing off as mine what is Bion's, but in the sense of writing the chapter as a chapter that reflects the ways I have been changed by Bion's paper, as opposed to what I have learned from it.[1]

"Notes on memory and desire" is an odd paper, only two and a half pages in length, initially published in 1967 in the first volume of a little-known journal, *The Psychoanalytic Forum*, which folded five years later. The paper entered the mainstream of psychoanalytic discourse only when it was reprinted fourteen years later in *Classics in psychoanalytic technique* (Langs, 1981), and twenty-one years later in *Melanie Klein today, Vol. 2: Mainly practice* (Spillius, 1988).

"Memory and desire" was one of Bion's late papers, written at a time when he had begun to suffer small strokes. After publishing this paper, Bion published only one major analytic work, *Attention and interpretation* (1970), and six very brief, relatively minor papers in the decade before his death in 1979.

I view "Memory and desire" as an unfinished paper, not because illness or death prevented Bion from completing it, but because it is a sketch, the beginnings of lines of thought of a sort that do not lend themselves to being completed, but that invite both elaboration and response.

This odd little paper is a landmark contribution. The significance of this paper lies not in its dictate to "cultivate a watchful avoidance of memory" (Bion, 1967a, p. 137) and to desist from "desires for results, 'cure,' or even understanding" (p. 137). To my mind, it proposes a revised analytic methodology. Bion supplants "awareness" from its central role in the analytic process and, in its place, instates the analyst's (largely unconscious) work of intuiting the psychic reality (the truth) of the session by becoming at one with it.

In the course of reading/rewriting "Memory and desire," I present a conception of temporality that I believe is more in keeping with Bion's revised methodology than the conception of the relationship that he offers in his paper. I offer two clinical examples that illustrate something of how I practice psychoanalysis, which is influenced by

---

1 This is a personal chapter, not a review of what others have done with Bion's paper. I find even the most original and perceptive rewritings of this paper by others (see Grotstein, 2009; Meltzer, 1978; Symington and Symington, 1996) to be distractions from my efforts to say what it is that *I make with Bion's paper* (as opposed to what I make *of* it).

Bion's "Memory and desire," but is not the way Bion practiced psychoanalysis, as reflected in the clinical and supervisory work he published (for example, Bion, 1959, 1987).

Sense impressions and unconscious thinking

Bion begins the paper with a series of direct statements that point out the unreliability of memory and desire as mental functions suitable for the analyst's use in his critical thinking and scientific judgment:

> Memory is always misleading as a record of fact since it is distorted by the influence of unconscious forces. (1967a, p. 136)

And the two sentences that follow:

> Desires interfere, by absence of mind when observation is essential, with the operation of judgment. Desires distort judgment by selection and suppression of material to be judged. (p. 136)

In the space of three concise sentences, Bion dismisses two large categories of mental functioning as unreliable for use by the psycho-analyst. Desires do not simply "interfere" with observation, they involve "absence of mind," a shutdown of genuine thinking. This is not a paper in which Bion rounds the edges. He immediately throws down the gauntlet.

In the second paragraph of the paper, Bion shifts to dense, enigmatic language:

> Memory and desire exercise and intensify those aspects of the mind that derive from sensuous experience. They thus promote capacity derived from sense impressions and designed to serve impressions of sense. They deal respectively with sense impressions of what is supposed to have happened and sense impressions of what has not yet happened. (p. 136)

Repeated readings of this paragraph fail to clarify meaning. I ask which "aspects of the mind" are "exercised and intensified" (such strange language) by memory and desire; what does it mean to "derive from sensuous experience" and "to serve impressions of sense"? I receive no reply to my questions from the text.

Finding that my usual methods of close reading are of no help here, I shift to a method of reading in which I allow unanswered questions to accrue until I begin to form impressions (as opposed to understandings)—impressions that suggest, but only suggest, meaning. It comes to mind as I grapple with these sentences that Bion is borrowing from Freud's (1911) "Formulations on the two principles of mental functioning" the term *sense impressions* (p. 220). "Two principles," which I consider to be the foundation of Freud's theory of thinking, is, I believe, the Freud paper to which Bion most often refers. This is not surprising, given that Bion's project, as I understand it, is the development of a psychoanalytic theory of thinking, which begins with "Experiences in groups" (Bion, 1947–1951) and runs through the entirety of the rest of his written and spoken work.

It would be a distraction to attempt to trace all the ways in which Bion adopts, rejects, and revises the ideas in Freud's paper, but there are two aspects of "Two principles" that I believe provide a necessary context for reading Bion's "Memory and desire." First, Freud views as "momentous" (1911, p. 219) the advance in early development when a new principle of mental functioning, the reality principle, begins to direct:

> . . . the psychical apparatus . . . to form a conception of the real circumstances in the external world and to endeavour to make a real alteration in them. (p. 219)

The second aspect of Freud's paper that forms an essential background for "Memory and desire" is the idea that the mind, under the dominance of the reality principle, employs a new form of action, the mental action of "*thinking*, which was developed from the presentation of ideas" (p. 221).

Thus, Freud places reality at the center of his theory of thinking, as does Bion. To my mind, Freud's concepts of the pleasure principle and the reality principle are the precursors of, and are still alive in, Bion's conception of mental operations that undermine, and mental operations that promote, an individual's ability to achieve and maintain footing in reality (truth). (In the spirit of Bion's paper, I would rename the reality principle and the pleasure principle *the truth-seeking principle* and *the truth-fearing principle*, respectively.)

If we look again at the dense second paragraph of "Memory and desire," with Freud's "Two principles" in mind, possible meanings present themselves. Once again, the paragraph begins:

Memory and desire exercise and intensify those aspects of the mind that derive from sensuous experience. They thus promote capacity derived from sense impressions and designed to serve impressions of sense. (Bion, 1967a, p. 136)

I would paraphrase this in the following way: memory and desire "exercise and intensify" those mental operations that have their origins in the response of the organism to sensory stimuli. Memory and desire enhance the power of the sense organs, which are "designed to serve [conscious] impressions of sense" and the power of the pleasure (truth-fearing) principle. In so doing, memory and desire undermine genuine unconscious thinking (and thereby contribute to "absence of mind").

The paragraph ends with the conclusion that memory and desire:

deal respectively with sense impressions of what is supposed to have happened and sense impressions of what has not yet happened. (p. 136)

In other words, memory and desire are mental operations that "deal with" (are irrevocably tied to) sense impressions and the pleasure (truth-fearing) principle, which cause memory to fashion the past as we wish it had been, and lead desire to treat the future as if we were able to foresee it and control it. For these reasons, memory and desire are antithetical to the goals of the psychoanalytic enterprise.

In my rewriting of "Memory and desire," I would like to make explicit what I believe to be implicit in the paragraph under discussion: *genuine thinking, which is predominantly unconscious, seeks out the truth (reality)*. This, I believe, is the core of Bion's theory of thinking. Moreover, sensory experience distracts from and undermines genuine thinking. Without the truth (O),[2] or at least openness to it, thinking is not only impossible; the very idea of thinking becomes meaningless, just as the readings of a compass are rendered meaningless in the absence of a North Pole.

It is important to note that Bion is unequivocal about the necessity to abstain from memory and desire. He intends to be shocking (in

---

2 "Since I don't know what that reality is [the truth of what is occurring in an analytic session], and since I want to talk about it, I have tried to deal with this position by simply giving it a symbol 'O' and just calling it 'O,' ultimate reality, the absolute truth" (Bion, 1967b, p. 136).

an effort, I believe, to shake up the solidly ensconced status quo of the then-current analytic methodologies). Nowhere else in his entire opus does Bion use language as strong as he does in "Memory and desire." Take, for instance, these dictates:

Obey the following rules:

1 *Memory*: Do not remember past meetings. . . .
2 *Desires*: Desires for results, "cures," or even understandings must not be allowed to proliferate. (p. 137)

And, later in the paper:

> The psychoanalyst should aim at achieving a state of mind so that at every session he feels he has not seen the patient before. If he feels he has, he is treating the wrong patient. (p. 138)

The reader should be stunned by these words. If he isn't stunned, he is reading the wrong paper. "How is it possible not to remember, and not to strive to understand?" the reader should emphatically respond. "And even if eschewing memory and desire were possible, which is doubtful, doesn't that detract greatly from analytic work? Isn't the analyst's act of holding in mind and remembering what the patient has said, sometimes for long periods of time, an important way in which the analyst holds together all the parts of the patient in a way that the patient may never before have been held together and recognized?"

Bion does not answer these questions directly. But I think that (it is always "I think," never "I know"), in the third paragraph of the paper, he begins to address the question of how analytic thinking may operate in the absence of the analyst's memory and desire:

> Psychoanalytic "observation" is concerned neither with what has happened nor with what is going to happen but with what *is* happening. (p. 136)

This is the first of what I believe to be the two most important statements that Bion makes in "Memory and desire." Analytic think-ing is concerned *only* with the present, with "what *is* happening," not with what *has* happened, or what *will* happen, thereby freeing the analyst of his dependence on memory and desire. Psychoanalysis is conducted solely in the present.

Bion adds:

> Furthermore, it [analytic "observation"] is not concerned with sense impressions or objects of sense. Any psychoanalyst knows depression, anxiety, fear and other aspects of psychic reality whether those aspects have been or can be successfully named or not. Of its reality he has no doubt. Yet anxiety, to take one example, has no shape, no smell, no taste. (p. 136)

This passage makes matters even more complex. Bion is now moving beyond the "rules" (p. 137) of eschewing memory and desire; he is saying that the analyst must refrain not only from memory and desire, but also from "sense impressions" and "objects of sense." He is separating emotions such as depression, anxiety, and fear from the sense impressions (the physical "accompaniments" [p. 136]) of emotions.

What seems crucial to me in this passage is the fact that Bion has returned to the question of reality. He says, "Any psychoanalyst knows depression, anxiety, fear and other aspects of psychic reality . . . These are the psychoanalyst's real world" (p. 136). Here Bion is making a plea for a distinctively psychoanalytic understanding of human experience in which there is a difference in the qualities of conscious and unconscious experience: "Any psychoanalyst knows . . . these are the psychoanalyst's real world."

The realm of the unconscious, Bion vehemently insists, is the realm of the psychoanalyst. No one knows the unconscious in the way that the psychoanalyst does, and he must protect it from being "confounded" (p. 137) with the conscious realm of experience. The unconscious is the realm of thinking and feeling that together form the psychic reality (psychoanalytic truth) of an individual at any given moment. The unconscious is not a realm of physical sensation. Physical sensation resides in the domain of conscious experience.

Intuiting psychic reality

All of what I have discussed so far sets the stage for the second of what I believe to be the two most crucial ideas that Bion presents in this landmark paper:

> Awareness of the sensuous accompaniments of emotional experience are a hindrance to the psychoanalyst's intuition of the reality with which he must be at one. (p. 136)

77

The idea Bion is presenting here runs counter to the notion that the analyst, while maintaining evenly floating attention, attempts to enhance as much as possible his "awareness" of all that is happening in both sensory and nonsensory dimensions of the session. For example, it is widely accepted that the analyst is interested in the "sensuous accompaniments" of his visual awareness of such events as the patient's gait as she walks to the couch, and in his olfactory awareness of the scent of perfume or perspiration in the consulting room, in the auditory awareness of music or cacophony or drone of the patient's voice, and so on.

Why, the reader might ask, would the analyst want to resist experiencing the sensuous accompaniments of emotions, the physicality of life in the consulting room? And how can any form of awareness of what is happening in the analytic setting be a "hindrance" to, and not an enhancement of, the analyst's receptivity to the patient's conscious and unconscious communications? I believe that a response, if not an answer, to these questions can be found in the final clause of the paragraph, where Bion states that the sensuous accompaniments of emotional experience are a hindrance to *"the psychoanalyst's intuition of the reality with which he must be at one"* (Bion, 1967a, p. 136, emphasis added).

In other words, if the psychoanalyst is to be genuinely analytic in the way he observes, he must be able to abjure conscious, sensory-based modes of perceiving, which draw the analyst's mind to conscious experience and to modes of thinking (for example, memory and desire) that are fearful/evasive of the perception of the unconscious psychic reality (the truth) of what is occurring in the session. Instead, the analyst must rely on a wholly different form of perceiving and thinking. That form of thinking, which Bion calls *intuition*, has its roots in the unconscious mind. Receptivity to sense impressions, "awareness," and "understanding" are the domain of conscious thought processes. For Bion (1962a), unconscious thinking is far richer than conscious (predominantly secondary process) thinking, which is required to conduct the business of waking life. The unconscious is free to view experience simultaneously from multiple vertices,[3] which

---

3 For Bion (1962a), unconscious thinking involves the viewing of experience from multiple perspectives simultaneously, thus generating a rich internal dialogue not possible in waking, conscious thinking. Modes of thinking that coexist in dialectical tension with one another include primary process and secondary process

would create havoc if one were to use such thinking while trying to carry out the tasks and conduct the interpersonal relationships of waking life.

This passage is something of an announcement that the task of the analyst is not that of understanding or figuring out the nature of the psychic reality of the moment in the analytic session; rather, the analyst's work is to intuit that unconscious psychic reality by becoming at one with it. Bion does not define the concept of intuition, nor does he offer a clinical illustration of it, but the term itself strongly suggests the predominance of unconscious mental processes in analytic thinking.

While the idea of intuiting the psychic reality of an experience by being at one with it may sound a bit mystical, I believe that we are all engaged in this sort of experience many times, each day, in our dream life. When we dream—both when we are asleep and when we are awake (Bion, 1962a)—we have the experience of sensing (intuiting) the reality of an aspect of our unconscious life and are at one with it. *Dreaming*, in the way I am using the term, is a transitive verb. In dreaming, we are not dreaming *about* something, we are *dreaming something*, "dreaming up" an aspect of ourselves. In dreaming, we are *at one* with the *reality* of the dream; we are the dream. While dreaming, we are intuiting (dreaming up) an element of our unconscious emotional lives, and we are at one with it in a way that differs from any other experience. In dreaming, we are most real to ourselves; we are most ourselves.

For me, reverie (Bion, 1962a, 1962b; Ogden, 1997), waking dreaming, is paradigmatic of the clinical experience of intuiting the psychic reality of a moment of an analysis. In order to enter a state of reverie, which in the analytic setting is always in part an intersubjective phenomenon (Ogden, 1994a), the analyst must engage in an act of self-renunciation. By self-renunciation, I mean the act of allowing oneself to become less definitively oneself in order to create a psychological space in which analyst and patient may enter into a shared state of intuiting and being-at-one-with a disturbing psychic reality that the patient, on his own, is unable to bear. The

---

thinking; the *container* and the *contained* (Bion 1962a); synchronic and diachronic senses of time; linear cause-and-effect thinking and pattern-based (field theory) thinking; paranoid-schizoid and depressive modes of generating experience; presymbolic and verbally symbolic forms of representing experience; and so on.

analyst does not seek reverie, any more than he seeks intuition. Reverie and intuition come, if they come at all, without effort, "unbidden" (Bion, 1967b, p. 147).

It is important to keep in mind that Bion is focusing in "Memory and desire" on one aspect of analytic methodology: the analyst's work of becoming intuitively at one with the patient's psychic reality. I would add—and I believe that Bion would agree (for instance, as reflected in the title of his book *Learning from experience* [1962a])— that psychoanalytic methodology is simultaneously involved in intuiting disturbing, unconscious psychic reality *and* in addressing the patient's fears of the truths of external reality. Among the frightening (and potentially enlivening) truths of external reality are the separateness of the lives of patient and analyst, and the absolute alterity of the world that lies beyond one's control.

Intuition, the known, and the unknown

Bion, in "Memory and desire," turns next to the relationship between intuition and the unknown:

> What is "known" about the patient is of no further consequence: it is either false or irrelevant. If it is "known" by patient and analyst, it is obsolete. . . . The only point of importance in any session is the unknown. Nothing must be allowed to distract from intuiting that. (1967a, p. 136)

To paraphrase, what is known has nothing further to offer and requires no further psychological work. It has yielded what it has to yield, and if patient or analyst continues to dwell on it, it fills psychological space in a "clogging" (p. 137), deadening way. What is known is "either false or irrelevant." It is irrelevant in that it no longer applies to what is happening now, even though it may have been relevant to what happened in yesterday's session or earlier in today's session. Analysis is concerned only with the present. It is false in that we use what we believe we "know" to create the illusion that the unknown is already known, thereby eliminating the need to deal with as-yet-unknown (troubling) psychic truths.

I would expand Bion's thinking about intuition in "Memory and desire" to include the idea that the work of intuition is manifested not simply in a deepened sense of the psychic reality of a given moment of an analysis but also, perhaps more important, is manifested in the ways patient and analyst have been changed by the experience of jointly becoming at one with the formerly unknown (and deeply troubling) psychic reality. I take something Bion (1967c) said in his Los Angeles seminars—which he conducted either shortly before or directly after he wrote "Memory and desire"—as a reflection of a similar idea. In the first of those seminars, he said:

> I think that what the patient is saying and what the interpretation is (which you give), is in a sense relatively unimportant. Because by the time you are able to give a patient an interpretation which the patient understands, all the work has been done. (1967c, p. 11)

I understand Bion to be saying that by that time the analyst is ready to make an interpretation, all the work has been done, in the sense that *the analyst and the patient have already been changed by the experience of jointly intuiting the unsettling psychic reality with which they have been at one.* The experience of coming to terms with, being at one with, a formerly unthinkable psychic reality changes both patient and analyst. The interpretation is superfluous. What is of importance when the analyst is ready to make an interpretation is the unknown, which is alive even as the analyst is making the interpretation of what is already known. That unknown "will not be interpreted probably for a long time . . . possibly even years" (p. 11).

The present moment of the past

Before presenting a clinical illustration of some of the concepts and phenomena I have been discussing, I will return, for a moment, to the starting point of my paper: the analyst's use of the mental operations of memory and desire.

I believe that Bion in "Memory and desire" makes too sharp a distinction between past and present, between remembering and living, when he makes categorical injunctions against remembering. It seems to me that Bion's conception of memory misconstrues the relationship of past and present, and the relationship between memory and current lived experience.

T. S. Eliot (1919) enriches our conception of the relationship of past to present when he writes that the past is always part of the present, a "present" that he calls "the present moment of the past" (p. 11). The present moment of the past, for a writer, is a present-time experience that contains the entire history of literature—a history "not of what is dead, but of what is already living" (p. 11). Similarly, in the analytic situation, the present in which patient and analyst live is a present that does not stand in contradistinction to a past that no longer exists; rather, the entirety of the past is alive in the present moment of the analytic experience. From this perspective, the analyst sacrifices nothing in eschewing memory. "The past is never dead. It's not even past" (Faulkner, 1950, act 1, scene 3).

Clinical illustration: A place for the baby

What I will offer here is a clinical example in which the patient and I were presented with an emotional problem that asked a good deal of us if we were to genuinely face and respond to what was happening at that moment in the analysis.

I had been working with Ms. C for several years in a five-sessions-per-week analysis when I began to feel, on meeting her in the waiting room, that she was in the wrong place, and that I should tell her politely that the person she came to see was located in another building on the same block as mine. This feeling was particularly puzzling because I was fond of Ms. C and almost always looked forward to seeing her for her sessions. When the patient lay down on the couch that same day, I had the impulse to say, "I love you."

After Ms. C told me a dream in which she had lost something but didn't know what she had lost, I said, "Is loving me such a terrible thing that you have to leave it somewhere else when you come to see me?" I had not planned to say this to the patient, but it felt true as I said it.

Without pause, Ms. C responded, "You've never told me that you love me before."

I said, "Would my love be in the wrong place if I were to love you?"

The patient said, "Yes, I think it would, but I would feel empty if I were to give it back."

I replied, again without pause, "As you were speaking, I couldn't tell whether you meant that you'd feel empty if you simply returned my love as something unwanted, something you had no use for, or whether you meant that feeling love for me would make you feel empty."

"I mean both. You shouldn't love me. I'm a patient. And I also feel that I love you, but I feel that it's being directed at no one, because you're here in form only, not as a real man I could go out with and possibly marry. That's not just a feeling, it's a fact that can't be undone."

I said, "When you tell me about 'facts that can't be undone,' I feel as if you're killing something or someone. You kill the person you love by saying I don't exist, and by saying I'm no one, so it's a waste of life to give me the love that you feel." I paused, and then said, "I think that in one way you'd like to hear me say, 'You and your love are in the right place. This is exactly the place for them.' But in another way, it would be terribly frightening if I were to say that."

Ms. C said, "I had a very disturbing dream last night in which I was holding my baby boy and saying, 'I love you,' but then I asked myself, 'Is that really true?' I felt that the truth was: no, I don't love him, and because of that he is going to die."

I said, "It's a savage thing that you do to yourself when you say to yourself and to me that you've killed your own child, and so your love for me can't be real. You're saying that a woman who killed her own baby is incapable of love, so the only thing to do with that love is to get rid of it, send it down the block to an imaginary person."

Ms. C said, "You're talking to me today in a way that makes me feel that I'm not an imaginary person, I'm a real person with . . ."

After a short while, I completed the sentence that I thought the patient had begun but could not complete: ". . . a real person with real love for another real person." I felt that Ms. C and I were engaged in a very intimate experience, the nature of which I could not name, but I felt deeply moved by it.

I am reluctant to dissect this moment in the analysis for fear of killing it with theory, but nonetheless I will try. The music of this session, as I listen to it now, is that of a love song intertwined with an elegy.

I sensed, when I met Ms. C in the waiting room, that she wanted to tell me that she genuinely loved her child who, in reality, had died *in utero* a year earlier, and that I, *as her child*, wanted to say the same ("I love you") to her. But I was not able to live with the anxiety stirred by this kind of thinking and feeling, so in my reverie experience, I sent those feelings down the block to an imaginary person. In retrospect, I think that I was frightened both by the intensity of the analytic love relationship in which Ms. C and I were engaged and by the intensity of the pain she would feel by my speaking to her *as her dead baby*.

The patient was married but had no living children. She had had a miscarriage (four and a half months into the pregnancy) and began analysis in the midst of a severe depression. She had ceased trying to have a baby after the miscarriage. Ms. C was convinced that her body was telling her that she was unfit to be a mother. She had no children, *and* she had one child who died when he was four and a half months old.

I felt deeply saddened by the patient's feelings of profound loss and guilt. When I spoke to Ms. C in the spontaneous way I have described, I was speaking of my love for her *as her dead baby*, without consciously thinking, "I'm speaking for the dead baby, *and* for the dead baby in the patient *and* for the dead baby in me." I simply spoke as myself, who at that moment was all three of the people I just mentioned. In doing so, I was at one with the psychic reality of the dead baby, which helped the patient to be at one with the reality of *her* dead baby, who was inseparable from me and from her deadened self.

The analytic experience that I have just described occurred, I believe, in the absence of memory. The reader will quite reasonably say, "Both you and Ms. C were remembering the patient's response to an actual miscarriage. You mentioned that fact only after you presented the clinical material, but I think that that fact belonged at the beginning of your presentation so that, as a reader, I could have had available to me the real historical context of the session as you presented your experience with this patient."

But I would say in response, "Neither the patient nor I was engaged in 'remembering the past,' but the past, the death of the baby, was nonetheless very much alive in the present moment of the analysis. You, the reader, may have felt confused about what was real and what was imaginary when I was telling you what happened in the session, but that confusion conveyed more of the truth of that moment of the analysis than would have been conveyed if I had provided the 'historical context' for what was happening. I think that if I had provided the 'real' historical context, I would have stripped the life from what was occurring in that moment of the analysis. Now that I think of it, I did give you a sense of the 'historical context' in the name I gave the clinical illustration: 'A place for the baby.' Perhaps, in giving that name to the clinical illustration, I was telling you, but not telling you, part of the emotional background of what was to follow, just as Ms. C and I both knew and did not know that what was happening between us was a way of feeling and talking about her experience of the death of her baby."

The analytic experience with Ms. C that I have described was built upon multiple coexisting, discordant realities, all of which were true: the baby was dead, *and* the baby was alive; the patient loved me, *and* the patient loved me as her baby; the patient loved her baby, *and* she felt incapable of loving him and unworthy of his love. The truth of each component of this emotional situation was real only when in dialectical tension with its counterpart. If I were to have sided with one component or the other (for instance, by saying, "You really did love your baby in the dream and the real baby who died"), I believe the patient would have felt that I was afraid to know who she really was at that moment: a mother who loved her baby, and a mother who was unable to love her baby.

Before ending this clinical discussion, I will comment briefly on the intertwined music of the elegy and the love song that, to my ear, runs through this segment of the analysis. The elegiac aspect involves primitive, undifferentiated forms of relatedness between the patient and me, between the patient and her dead baby, and between the baby and me. Ms. C and I were experiencing a wide range of deeply felt emotions concerning the dead baby, the origins of which were unclear: were they my feelings, or were they the patient's feelings, or were they those of a third subject that was an unconscious creation of the two of us (which I have elsewhere called the *analytic third* [Ogden, 1994b])? Probably all three, in ever-shifting proportions.

At the same time, and in dialectical tension with the elegy, the music of the love song involves more mature forms of relatedness in which Ms. C's and my own sense of alterity to one another is integral to the intense feelings of intimacy, mutual understanding, and even a sense of danger in what was happening in "the analytic love relationship." I use the term *analytic love relationship* not to suggest that the love is less real than in other love relationships, but to specify that this form of love relationship is conceived, and develops within, the very real constraints of the doctor–patient relationship (the analytic frame).

Evolution and interpretation

Following his comments on intuitive thinking and being at one with the psychic reality of the present moment, Bion, in "Memory and desire," introduces the concept of *evolution,* the meanings of which remain obscure in the paper, I think intentionally so:

In any session, evolution takes place. Out of the darkness and form-lessness something evolves. This evolution can bear a superficial resemblance to memory, but once it has been experienced it can never be confounded with memory. It shares with dreams the quality of being wholly present or unaccountably and suddenly absent. This evolution is what the psychoanalyst must be ready to interpret. (1967a, pp. 136–137)

Bion seems to be using the term *evolves* to refer to what is happening in the analytic experience: the emotional experience that is occurring. The term *evolution* here is more verb than noun. It is a state of continuous change, and that process of change is the subject of psychoanalysis.

As I mentioned earlier, the analytic inquiry in "Memory and desire" is focused exclusively on the present moment of the past. Bion's methodology transforms the most fundamental clinical question from "What does that mean?" to "What's happening now?" The question "What does that mean?" lies at the core of Freud's (1900) work with dreams and Klein's (1975) search for symbolic meaning in children's play. Winnicott (1971), who shifted the focus of child and adult analysis from the symbolic content of play to the capacity for playing, is, I believe, as important a contributor as Bion to the alteration of the fundamental clinical question to "What's happening now?"

The passage introducing the concept of evolution, quoted above, brings to mind an experience I have had innumerable times while being told a dream by a patient. As the analysand is telling me the dream, I usually have no trouble imagining the scene or scenes being described. But I find that as soon as the patient has finished telling me the dream (and sometimes even while the patient is telling me a dream), I have no recollection at all of what the patient has told me. This experience underscores the fact that dreams that patients tell us are not memories; they are experiences evolving in the present moment of the analysis and have many of the qualities of dreaming, including that oft-experienced surprise and disappointment of finding that the dream, which a moment ago was so present and alive, is "unaccountably and suddenly absent" (Bion, 1967a, p. 137). No amount of conscious concentration will bring it back. Often, I find that later in the session, the patient's dream will come to me "unbidden."

For me, one of the most important words in this paragraph on evolution is the final word of the closing sentence: *interpret.*

"This evolution is what the psychoanalyst must be ready to interpret" (p. 137). Bion suggests that he is using the term *interpret* to refer to the analyst's talking to the patient about the psychic reality that is occurring (now) in the present moment of the analysis. He gives no clue as to what that might sound like. I can only say what the term *interpret* means to me. But instead of trying to define, or even describe its meaning, I will let the following clinical account speak for itself before I try to attach words to it.

Clinical illustration: An invitation to stay

When I opened the door to the waiting room, it seemed more starkly furnished than I'd remembered. There were four magazines, all of them many months out of date, lying on the table that had sat there for more than twenty years.

Ms. J didn't make eye contact with me as she rose from her chair, as if lifting a tremendous weight. She slowly led the way into my consulting room.

After lying down on the couch, she said in a flat voice, "I got up and made sandwiches for the kids. I put the milk and cereal on the breakfast table and somehow got them to school. I can do that."

I felt that Ms. J was very close to losing her mind as well as her ability to function, which frightened me. But I was frightened more for Ms. J's children than I was for her. I pictured them staring at her at the breakfast table, pretending not to notice the lifeless expression on her face.

I said, "As you talk, I'm reminded of the instructions they give on airplanes to put on your own oxygen mask before helping your child to put theirs on."

Ms. J said, "I was looking at a photo that I have framed on my dresser. It's a photo of Jane when she was about six, holding Lisa, who was only a few months old. The expression on Jane's face is the thing that grabs my attention every time I look at it. She has a pleading look in her eyes that says, 'I don't want to drop her. Please take her from me. I'm too young to be holding a baby.' When I look at that picture, it makes me want to cry. I saw, when I looked at it this morning, that Jane wasn't looking at me or pleading with me, she was looking somewhere else."

I said, "That's the weight you have to carry that's too heavy for you, and would be too heavy for anyone—the weight of the secret that you're not there in the photograph, you're not there in the waiting room when I meet you, you're not here when you're lying on the couch, you're not anywhere."

Ms. J said, "I went to the Diebenkorn exhibit at the Museum of Modern Art. I went to kill time."

I said, "You didn't have to go to the exhibit to kill time. I think that you're already dead, so you don't have time to kill; that's the thing dead people don't have time. When you're in the waiting room, I don't think you're waiting to begin the session—you know nothing is going to happen, so there's nothing to wait for."

Ms. J said, "I stopped wearing a watch months ago, maybe a year. I didn't decide not to wear one, I just found that I didn't have one on, and I haven't put one on since then. I have one on my dresser, and I could put it on in the morning, but I don't, and I've never missed it." As Ms. J was telling me this, it seemed to me that she was mildly interested in what she was saying, which was a rare thing.

"Is it time for me to go?" she asked, her voice now flat again.

Without knowing what I was going to say, I said, "No, it's time for you to stay." Ms. J smiled, faintly.

On hearing what I had just said to Ms. J, it felt true, not simply in a concrete sense—it was not yet the time designated for the end of the session—it was true in an emotional sense. I felt I was inviting her—not just anybody, but her in particular—to stay and spend time with me, "living time," as opposed to clock time, or photograph time, or obligatory time, or dead time, or killing time. I genuinely wanted to spend time with her. I liked her, even enjoyed her, and was inviting her to stay.

For me, the "invitation" was the most important "interpretation" that I made in that session. What I said to Ms. J was my way of conveying my sense of the psychic reality that was most alive at that moment. The "invitation" I gave her to spend "living time" with me was not a request to have her do something with me in the future; it was my way of saying to Ms. J that we were already, in that moment, spending living time with one another. Her smile was not her acceptance of my invitation so much as it was her acknowledgment that something was already happening in which she was present.

I believe that there are important similarities between what I have just said about what occurred in the session with Ms. J and what Bion is referring to when he says, "This evolution is what the psychoanalyst must be ready to interpret." But the word *interpret*, for me, holds the connotation of the analyst telling the patient what he understands to be the unconscious meaning of what the patient is saying or doing. I would prefer a different term—a term that does not carry that connotation—to describe what I was doing when I spontaneously said, "No, it's time for you to stay." A "term" that would feel more apt, although wordy, would be: *talking with the patient, directly or indirectly, about what is most real and most alive at an unconscious level at that moment.* Most often, this type of "talking with a patient" does not sound like a psychoanalyst making "an interpretation." To me, it sounds and feels like two people talking to one another, two people conversing. I take it as high praise when a patient says to me, "You never make interpretations, you just talk to me."

The purpose of talking with patients is multifold, but for me, it always includes the effort to help the patient become more fully alive to his or her experience in the present moment. As Bion puts it toward the end of "Memory and desire":

> "Progress" will be measured by the increased number and variety of moods, ideas and attitudes seen in any given session. (1967a, p. 137)

The analytic conversation that evolves with each patient is unique to that patient, and could not occur between any other two people in the world. These are some of the qualities of my way of talking with patients (what Bion calls *interpreting*). The way I talk with patients is not the way any other analyst talks with patients; if it were, the patient would be talking with the wrong analyst.

Concluding comments

Bion's "Notes on memory and desire" (1967a) is an impossible paper that I have struggled with for decades. Despite its title, it is not, most importantly, a paper about memory and desire. The significance of this paper lies in the way it supplants awareness from its central role in the analytic process, and in its place, instates the analyst's (largely unconscious) work of intuiting the (unconscious) psychic reality of the present moment by becoming at one with it.

The clinical examples from my own work illustrate something of my own manner of being at one with the psychic reality (the truth) of a given moment of a session, and my ways of talking with the patient about that reality.

References

Bion, W. R. (1948–1951). Experiences in groups. In *Experiences in groups and other papers* (pp. 29–141). New York: Basic Books, 1959.

Bion, W. R. (1959). Attacks on linking. *International Journal of Psychoanalysis*, 40, 308–315.

Bion, W. R. (1962a). *Learning from experience*. London: Basic Books.

Bion, W. R. (1962b). A theory of thinking. In *Second thoughts* (pp. 110–119). New York: Aronson, 1967.

Bion, W. R. (1967a). Notes on memory and desire. In J. Aguayo and B. Malin (eds), *Wilfred Bion: Los Angeles seminars and supervision* (pp. 136–138). London: Karnac, 2013.

Bion, W. R. (1967b). Author's response to discussions of "Notes on memory and desire." In J. Aguayo and B. Malin (eds), *Wilfred Bion: Los Angeles seminars and supervision* (pp. 136–138). London: Karnac, 2013.

Bion, W. R. (1967c). First seminar—12 April 1967. In J. Aguayo and B. Malin (eds), *Wilfred Bion: Los Angeles seminars and supervision* (pp.1–31). London: Karnac, 2013.

Bion, W. R. (1970). *Attention and interpretation*. London: Tavistock.

Bion, W. R. (1987). Clinical seminars. In F. Bion (ed.), *Clinical seminars and other works* (pp. 1–240). London: Karnac.

Eliot, T. S. (1919). Tradition and individual talent. In *Selected essays* (pp. 3–11). New York: Harcourt, Brace & World, 1960.

Faulkner, W. (1950). *Requiem for a nun*. New York: Vintage.

Freud, S. (1900). The interpretation of dreams. *S. E.*, 4/5.

Freud, S. (1911). Formulations on the two principles of mental functioning. *S. E.*, 12.

Grotstein, J. S. (2009). "*. . . But at the same time and on another level . . .*": *Psychoanalytic theory and technique in the Kleinian/Bionian mode, Vol. 1*. London: Karnac.

Klein, M. (1975). *Envy and gratitude and other works, 1946–1963*. New York: Delacorte Press/Seymour Lawrence.

Langs, R. (ed.). (1981) *Classics in psychoanalytic technique* (pp. 269–271). New York: Aronson.

Meltzer, D. (1978). The bondage of memory and desire. In *The Kleinian development, Part III: The clinical significance of the work of Bion* (pp. 269–271). Perthshire, Scotland: Clunie Press.

Ogden, T. H. (1994a). Projective identification and the subjugating third. In *Subjects of analysis* (pp. 97–106). Northvale, NJ: Aronson.

Ogden, T. H. (1994b). The analytic third—working with intersubjective clinical facts. *International Journal of Psychoanalysis*, 75, 3–20.

Ogden, T. H. (1997). Reverie and interpretation. *Psychoanalytic Quarterly*, 66, 567–595.

Spillius, E., (ed.) (1988). *Melanie Klein today, Vol. 2: Mainly practice: Developments in theory and practice* (pp. 15–18). London: Routledge.

Symington, J. and Symington, N. (1996). Without memory and desire. In *The clinical thinking of Wilfred Bion* (pp. 166–174). New York: Brunner Routledge.

Winnicott, D. W. (1971). *Playing and reality*. New York: Basic Books.

5

ON BECOMING A
PSYCHOANALYST[1]

Few of us feel that we really know what we are doing when we complete our formal psychoanalytic training. We flounder. We strive to find our "voice," our own "style," a feeling that we are engaging in the practice of psychoanalysis in a way that bears our own watermark. "It is only after you have qualified [as an analyst] that you have a chance of becoming an analyst. The analyst you become is you and you alone; you have to respect the uniqueness of your own personality—that is what you use, not all these interpretations [these theories that you use to combat the feeling that you are not really an analyst and do not know how to become one]" (Bion, 1987, p.15).

In this chapter we discuss a variety of maturational experiences that have been important to us in our own efforts to become analysts following our analytic training. Of course, the types of experience that were of particular value to each of us were different, but they also overlapped in important ways. We try to convey both the commonality of, and the differences between, the sorts of experience that have been most significant to us in our efforts to become (to mature as) analysts. In addition, we discuss several defensive measures that analysts in general, and we in particular, have made use of in the face of the anxiety that is inherent to the process of genuinely becoming an analyst in one's own terms.

---

1 This chapter was co-authored with Glen O. Gabbard, MD.

A theoretical context

A variety of experiences throughout one's development as an analyst are fundamental to one's maturation as both an analyst and an individual. The maturation of the analyst has much in common with psychic development in general. We have identified four aspects of psychic growth that are essential to our view of the process of becoming an analyst.

The first is the idea that thinking/dreaming one's lived experience in the world constitutes a principal means, perhaps the principal means, by which one learns from experience and achieves psychological growth (Bion, 1962a). Moreover, one's lived experience often is so disturbing as to exceed the individual's capacity to do anything with it psychically, i.e., to think or dream it. Under such circumstances, it requires two people to think or dream the experience. The psychoanalysis of each of our patients inevitably places us in situations that we have never before experienced and, as a result, requires of us a larger personality than that which we have brought to the analysis. We view this as true of every analysis: there is no such thing as an "easy" or "straightforward" analysis. The reconceptualization of pro-jective identification as an intrapsychic/interpersonal process in the writings of Bion (1962a, 1962b) and Rosenfeld (1987) recognizes that in these novel, disturbing analytic situations, the analyst requires another person to help make the unthinkable thinkable. That other person is most often the patient, but may be a supervisor, colleague, mentor, consultation group, and so on.

Inherent in this notion of intersubjective thinking is the idea that throughout the life of the individual, "it takes [at least] two people to make one" (Bion, 1987, p. 222). It requires a mother-and-infant capable of helping the infant to achieve "unit status" (Winnicott, 1958a, p. 44). It takes three people—mother, father, and child—to create a healthy oedipal child; it takes three people—mother, father, and adolescent—to create a young adult; it takes two young adults to create a psychological space in which to create a couple that is, in turn, capable of creating a psychological space in which a baby can be conceived (literally and metaphorically); it takes a combination of a young family and an old one (a grandmother, grandfather, mother, father, and child) to create conditions that contribute to, or facilitate the acceptance and creative use of, the experience of aging and death in the grandparents (Loewald, 1979).

However, this intersubjective conception of the development of the analyst is incomplete in the absence of its intrapsychic counterpart. This brings us to the second aspect of the theoretical context for this discussion: in order to think/dream our own experience, we need periods of personal isolation no less than we need the participation of the minds of others. Winnicott (1963) recognized this essential developmental requirement when he noted, "There is an intermediate stage in healthy development in which the patient's most important experience in relation to the good or potentially satisfying object is the refusal of it" (p. 182). In the analytic setting, the psychological work that is done between the sessions is no less important than the work done with the analyst in the sessions. Indeed, analyst and patient need to "sleep on" the session—i.e., they need to dream it on their own before they are able to do further work as an analytic pair. Similarly, in the sessions, the psychological work that the patient does in isolation from the analyst (and that the analyst does in his isolated space behind the couch) is as important as the thinking/dreaming that the two do with one another. These dimensions—the interpersonal and the solitary—are fully interdependent and stand in dialectical tension with one another. (When we speak of personal isolation, we are referring to a psychological state different from the state of being alone in the presence of another person—i.e., Winnicott's [1958b] "capacity to be alone." Rather, what we have in mind is a state that is much less dependent on external, or even internalized, object relations [see Ogden, 1991, for a discussion of this healthy state of "personal isolation"].)

The third aspect of psychic growth that is essential to our conception of maturation in the analyst is the idea that becoming an analyst involves a process of "dreaming oneself more fully into existence" (Ogden, 2004a, p. 858) in progressively more complex and inclusive ways. In the tradition of Bion (1962a), we are using the term "*dreaming*" to refer to the most profound form of thinking. It is a type of thinking in which the individual is able to transcend the limits of secondary process logic without loss of access to that form of logic. Dreaming occurs continuously, both during sleep and during waking life. Just as the stars persist even when their light is obscured by the light of the sun, so, too, dreaming is a continuous function of the mind that continues during waking life, even though obscured from consciousness by the glare of waking life. (Waking dreaming in the analytic setting takes the form of the analyst's reverie experience [Bion, 1962a; Ogden, 1997].) The timelessness of dreams allows one to simultaneously elaborate a multiplicity of perspectives on an emotional experience in a way that is not possible in the context of linear time and cause-and-effect logic that characterize waking, secondary process thinking. (The simultaneity of multiple perspectives that was captured in the cubist art of Picasso and Braque has had an influence on twentieth-century art of every genre—the poetry of T. S. Eliot and Ezra Pound, the novels of Faulkner and the late novels of Henry James, the plays of Harold Pinter and Ionesco, and the films of Kieslowski and David Lynch, as well as the art of psychoanalysis.)

The work of dreaming is the psychological work through which we create personal, symbolic meaning, thereby becoming ourselves. It is in this sense that we dream ourselves into existence as analysts, analysands, supervisors, parents, friends, and so on. In the absence of dreaming, we cannot learn from our lived experience and consequently remain trapped in an endless, unchanging present.

The fourth aspect of psychic growth that we believe to be fundamental to the way we think about the process of becoming an analyst is Bion's (1962a, 1970) concept of the container-contained. The "container" is not a thing but a process of doing psychological work with our disturbing thoughts. The term "doing psychological work" is roughly equivalent to such ideas/feelings as the experience of "coming to terms with" an aspect of one's life that has been difficult to acknowledge, or "making one's peace with" important, deeply disturbing events in one's life, such as the death of a parent, a child, a spouse, or one's own approaching death. The "contained" is the psychological representation of what one is coming to terms with or making one's peace with. The breakdown of a mutually generative relationship between thoughts derived from disturbing experience (the contained) and the capacity to think/dream those thoughts (the container) may take a number of forms, which manifest themselves in a variety of types of failure to mature as an analyst (Ogden, 2004b). The disturbing lived experiences—"the contained" (for example, boundary violations on the part of the analyst's personal analyst) may destroy the analyst's capacity for thinking as an analyst ("the container"), particularly under certain emotional circumstances (Gabbard and Lester, 1995).

With these ideas in mind, we will now consider a set of maturational experiences that are common to analysts in the course of their development. When one completes psychoanalytic training, one often has the vague sense of feeling a bit fraudulent. One is authorized to "fly solo" without the help of a supervisor, yet one feels a degree of turbulence that can be disconcerting. At times, analysts welcome the opportunity to learn from (and mature in) the sorts of analytic situations that we are about to describe. At other times, under other circumstances, analysts suddenly and inadvertently find themselves immersed in these disturbing analytic situations and achieve psychological growth by means of "flying by the seat of their pants."

Maturational experiences of the analyst

In the sections of the paper that follow, we discuss a number of types of maturational experience that have played an important role in the development of our analytic identities. These experiences include the gradual process of developing one's own way of speaking with patients; developing one's sense of oneself as an analyst in the course of presenting clinical work to a consultant; making self-analytic use of experiences with patients; and creating/discovering oneself as an analyst in the process of writing analytic papers.

Developing a voice of one's own

In listening to oneself speak (for example, to one's patients, super-visees, colleagues, and seminar members), one asks oneself, "What do I sound like when I speak like that?" "Do I really want to sound like that?" "Who do I sound like?" "In what ways do I sound foreign to the person I have become and am becoming?" "If I were to speak differently, what might that sound like?" "How would it feel to speak in a way that is different from anyone other than me?" There is a paradox in the fact that speaking naturally, as oneself, is both easy (in the sense of not having to pretend to be someone other than oneself) and very difficult (in the sense of finding/inventing a voice that emerges from the totality of who one is at a given moment). When paying close attention, one discovers that there are unmistakable residues of one's analyst's voice in the words spoken to one's patients. These ways of speaking are "in our bones," internalized long ago and made part of us without our being aware of the assimilation process.

While this mode of maturational experience largely occurs in the context of speaking to others, there is also an intrapsychic aspect, a conscious and unconscious battle with oneself in the effort to find/create oneself as an analyst. The voices one hears are largely in one's head (Smith, 2001), and belong to our "ghosts" and "ancestors" (Loewald, 1960, p. 249). The ghosts inhabit us in a way that is not fully integrated into our sense of self; our ancestors provide us with a sense of continuity with the past. In the process of becoming an analyst, we must "dream up" for ourselves an authentic way of speaking that involves disentangling ourselves from our own analyst(s), as well as from past supervisors, teachers, and writers we admire, while also drawing on what we have learned from them. A dialectical tension exists between inventing oneself freshly, on the one hand, and creatively using one's emotional ancestry, on the other.

No one has described better than Loewald, the psychological dilemmas that are involved in the passage of authority from one generation to the next. In "The waning of the Oedipus complex," Loewald (1979) describes the ways in which growing up (becoming a mature individual in one's own right) requires that one simultaneously kill one's parents (in more than a metaphoric way) and immortalize them. The parricide is an act of claiming one's own place as a person responsible for oneself and to oneself; the immortalizing of one's parents (an act of atonement ["at-one-ment"] for the parricide) involves a metamorphic internalization of the parents. This internalization is "metamorphic" in that the parents are not simply transformed into an aspect of oneself (a simple identification). Rather, it is an internalization of a far richer sort: that of incorporating into one's own identity a version of the parents that includes a conception of who they might have become but were unable to become, as a consequence of the limitations of their own personalities and the circumstances in which they lived. What better atonement can one make to the parents one kills (Ogden, 2006)?

In the process of becoming an analyst, one must be able to commit acts of parricide in relation to one's own analytic parents, while atoning for the parricide in the act of internalizing a transformed version of them. That metamorphic internalization recognizes their strengths and weaknesses and involves an incorporation into one's identity of a sense not only of who they were, but also of who they might have become, had external and internal circumstances allowed.

In the following clinical vignette, one of us (T.H.O) describes an experience in which patient and analyst together lived and dreamt an experience that facilitated maturation on both their parts.

For a significant period of time, the analyst found himself using the word "Well" to introduce virtually every question and comment that he addressed to his patients. It felt so natural that it took him a long time to recognize the fact that he had adopted this pattern of speech. He also noticed that he spoke in this way only while talking with patients and not while speaking with supervisees, conversing in seminars, talking with colleagues, and so on. On becoming aware that he was speaking in this way, it was immediately apparent to him that he had adopted a mannerism of his first analyst. He felt no need to "correct it" since, he told himself, he experienced it as an emotional connection with a man he liked and admired. What he did not realize was that he also saw no need to look into it (i.e., to think about why this identification had evidenced itself in that form at that juncture in his life and at that juncture in his work with these particular patients).

One of the patients with whom he was working in analysis during this period was Mr. A, a man who had chosen a career in the same field in which his father was a prominent figure. It was in the sessions with this patient—though there were related experiences with other patients—that he began to feel differently about what had seemed to him a harmless quirk in his manner of speech. This shift in perspective came over a period of weeks as he listened to Mr. A minimize the effect on him of having entered the same field as his father while at the same time repeatedly using the phrase "his field" instead of "my field" or "our field." During this period of the analysis, Mr. A mentioned an instance in which it seemed to the analyst that the patient was very uncharacteristically teasing one of his children for "trying to act like a grown-up." Even though the analyst did not comment on the behavior, it had a disturbing effect on him.

At the beginning of a session during this period of work, the patient complained that the analyst was making too much of the effects of his choice to go into "my father's field." The analyst believed that he had been careful not to take sides on the matter, so he chose to remain silent in response to his patient's accusation. Later in the session, Mr. A told the following dream: "An earthquake had begun with just a few short bursts, but I knew that this was just the beginning of an enormous earthquake in which I could very well be killed. I tried to gather a few things that I would like to take with me before getting out of the house that I was in. It was kind of like my house. I reached for a family photograph—one that I actually have on a table in my living room. It's a photo I took in Florida of my parents, Karen [his wife], and the kids. I felt an enormous pressure of time—it felt as if I was suffocating, and that it was crazy to spend the last breath of air I had on saving the photograph. Suffocation isn't the way an earthquake gets you, but that was how I felt. I woke up frightened, with my heart pounding." (For reasons that were not at all apparent to the analyst, he, too, felt intensely anxious as the patient told the dream.)

In the course of talking about the dream, Mr. A was struck by the fact that "because I took the photograph, I wasn't in the picture. I was in it as an observer, not as a member of the cast." The analyst said, "You were initially frightened by the feeling of the beginnings of an earthquake that might increase in force to the point that it might well kill you and everything that is dear to you; later in the dream, you felt that you were one breath away from dying by suffocation. I think that you were talking with yourself and with me in the dream about your feeling that you are being squeezed out of your own life— you were only an observer in the family picture, and yet you were willing to use your last breath of air to preserve for yourself even that marginal place. That seemed crazy to you even in the dream."

As the analyst was saying this, it occurred to him that Mr. A, in his telling of the dream, may have been making an observation about the analyst. The patient's saying that he knew that he "could very well be killed" by the earthquake involved a phrasing that not only used the same word on which the analyst was focused, but also linked it directly to the idea of being killed. This led the analyst to suspect that Mr. A was responding to something happening in the analyst that was reflected in the change in his manner of speech. It seemed to him that the patient was afraid that the analyst had developed a form of verbal tic that reflected a craziness in the analyst that would prevent him from being the analyst whom he needed. If the analyst, too, were being squeezed out of his own life as an analyst and his own way of speaking (with which the patient had become familiar over the years), how could the analyst be of help to him with a very similar problem?

The analyst thought that it was highly unlikely that the telling of this dream was Mr. A's first unconscious comment on something he perceived to be significantly different in the analyst's way of speaking. The patient's dream was critical to the analytic work, not because it was addressing feelings so very different from those being addressed in other dreams, but because it was the first time that the analyst was able to hear and respond to what he believed to be the patient's unconscious effort to talk to him about his fear that he perceived an ominous change in the analyst. In retrospect, the source of the symptom (as the analyst came to understand it) had affected his ability to mature as a person and as an analyst. Also in hindsight, the analyst recognized that the patient's cruelly pointing out his child's "trying to act like a grown-up" represented a communication to the analyst regarding the patient's self-hatred for the ways he felt like a child. (We view the dream as a dream that cannot be ascribed to the patient alone, but to an unconscious subject that is co-constructed by patient and analyst—"the analytic third" [Ogden, 1994]. It is this third subject that dreams the problems in the analytic relationship [in addition to the patient and analyst as individual dreamers].)

The patient's unconscious observation that he was an observer in the family photo, in conjunction with the analyst's awareness of his own anxiety while listening to the dream, led the analyst to begin a line of thought, a conversation with himself, about the meanings of his imitation of his first analyst. What was most powerful about the new awareness of the speech pattern that he had adopted was its persistence and invariability across the full range of emotional situations and across very different kinds of conversations with very different sorts of patients. It seemed to him that the impersonal quality of this generic way of speaking reflected a subliminal feeling that he had harbored for a very long time, but had not previously put into words for himself: It had seemed to him during his first analysis (and subsequently) that his analyst had in some important ways perceived him in generic ways that were neither personal to him nor to the analyst. There was a way in which he felt that his first analyst's perception of him was unwavering and missing something important. Both of these feelings were reflected in the photograph in the dream in that the photograph, too, was unchanging and did not include the photographer. The analyst felt some disappointment in his first analyst, but primarily felt ashamed that he had not had the courage to consciously recognize the impersonal quality of the way he felt he was being perceived and to register a protest. In the dream, there was a choice between the dreamer's saving the photograph and saving his own life. The analyst realized that he had metaphorically chosen to save the photograph—his fixed image of his own analyst—and, as a consequence, had given up something of his own vitality.

On the basis of these thoughts and others that followed in the succeeding weeks and months, the analyst was eventually able to speak with Mr. A about Mr. A's feelings of shame (the shame of having betrayed himself) in having chosen to pursue a career in "his father's field" and not a career in his own field (even if it was the field in which his father also worked). (We will return to this clinical example later in the chapter.)

Presenting clinical material to a consultant

When struggling with a clinical situation in one's practice, analysts frequently turn to a trusted colleague. Listening to oneself in this context is significantly different from those instances in which one speaks to patients, students, or supervisees. Analysts, in speaking with a consultant, are not attempting to understand the other person as they would in their work with a patient. The gradient of maturity (Loewald, 1960) tilts in the other direction in an analyst's work with a consultant. The analyst's insecurities and anxieties are center stage, given the fact that he has explicitly requested the help of the consultant. The emphasis is on what the analyst does NOT know. The analyst's lack of understanding—his self-doubt, anxiety, dread, shame, guilt, boredom, blind spots, lust, envy, hate, and terror—are all exposed to a colleague in an act of faith. The experience of one's own limits (as an analyst and as a person), and the acceptance of those limits by the consultant, help shape the analyst's identity in the direction of humility, curiosity about himself, and the awareness that his own analysis is a lifelong task. A portion of the analyst's identity involves conflict, ambivalence, longings, and fears from childhood, and an attempt to come to terms with the fact that the analyst's personal analysis has not allowed him to transcend the internal torment that drew him to analytic work in the first place. Moreover, the fact that the consultant does not recoil in response to the analyst's struggles provides confirmation that being "good enough," in Winnicott's (1951, p. 237) terms, is acceptable to others, and that the analyst will inevitably fall short of the comprehensive understanding and therapeutic results for which he may strive.

Aspects of the analyst's lived experience exceed his capacity to do psychological work with them and often emerge in the context of his encounters with his patients. Seeking out consultation may provide a much-needed container when an analyst finds it impossible to process what he is confronting, both in himself and in his patients. One of us (G.O.G.) worked for years with a relentlessly suicidal patient who continued to plan her suicide despite the analyst's best efforts to understand, contain, and interpret the multiple motives and meanings involved in the wish to die.

After the analyst presented this dilemma to a consultant, the consultant noted that the analyst was attempting to ward off the idea that all of his well-intentioned efforts were likely to come to naught, and the patient would probably end her life in spite of the treatment. The consultant stressed that the analyst was exasperated with the patient's interpersonally enacted fantasy of having omnipotent control over him and with his own inability to accept his powerlessness to prevent the patient from committing suicide. Ultimately, suicide would be the patient's choice without regard for the analyst's desires or needs. Hearing the consultant's comments allowed the analyst to work with these frightening thoughts and provided a way of detoxifying them so they could actually be thought by the analyst, accepted as inherent to the treatment situation, and heard as a communication of the patient's own feeling of not having a say about her own life or death.

The analyst's mind had been colonized by the patient's internal world, and as that colonization diminished, the analyst became aware that his own aspirations for the analytic enterprise were being thwarted by the patient's unwavering death wish (Gabbard, 2003). Like many analysts, he harbored a powerful unconscious fantasy regarding the analytic relationship—one in which a specific form of object relationship would be generated. He would be the devoted, selfless healer, and the patient would progressively improve and ultimately express gratitude to the analyst for his help (Gabbard, 2000). His suicidal patient had not agreed to this unconscious contract, and her march toward self-destruction continued in spite of—or perhaps oblivious to— the analyst's wish to help. With further reflection, the analyst recognized that he had been relegated to a transference position that would later be described by Steiner (2008) as the excluded observer who resents the fact that he is not the primary object for the patient.

The consultation also freed up the analyst to reflect on resonances from earlier developmental experiences in which he had realized his powerlessness in the face of the inevitable decline and death of others and himself, an important unconscious determinant of his career choice. Looking squarely at his magical wishes, and recognizing the impossibility of determining what another human being (or he himself) ultimately will do, constituted pivotal elements of the maturation of the analyst. Part of knowing who one is as an analyst is knowing the limits of one's power to influence a patient and using that knowledge to be able to listen and respond to a patient who confronts her own limits (as well as those of the analyst).

One's analytic work as a principal medium for self-analysis

Every analysis is incomplete. As Freud (1937) stressed, termination is ordinarily a practical matter rather than a definitively determined endpoint marked by conflict resolution. It is widely accepted now that we do not "terminate" an analysis (with a belief that we have helped the patient achieve a "complete" analysis); rather, the patient and analyst end an experience in analysis at a point at which they feel that a significant piece of psychological work has been achieved, and that they are at a juncture at which the principal work at hand feels to them to be that of their separation. Put still differently: transference is interminable, countertransference is interminable, conflict is interminable. A generative experience in analysis sets a process in motion that will continue throughout the patient's life.

The analyst's self-analysis serves a contrapuntal function to the dialogue one has with a trusted consultant. The interpersonal experience of working with the consultant is punctuated by periods of isolation in which one thinks one's own thoughts in the quiet of one's car, in the wee hours of the morning when one is staring at the ceiling, or in the privacy of one's consulting room while waiting for a patient who does not appear. Psychoanalytic treatment initiates an exploration—often tentative and ambivalent—of the inner life of both patient and analyst. Self-analysis contributes to that process, but in this variation one works alone, determined to look unflinchingly at what one finds, but always falling short of the mark. From this perspective, the ending of an analysis, the "end" of a piece of self-analytic work or of analytic work with a consultant, is not the point at which unconscious conflict is resolved, but the point at which the subject of the analytic work is able to think and dream his experience (to a large degree) for himself.

Discovering/creating what one thinks and who one is in the experience of writing

Writing is a form of thinking. Very often, in writing, one does not write what one thinks; one thinks what one writes. There is something of the feeling that ideas come out of one's pen, of watching ideas develop in unplanned ways (Ogden, 2005). Writing, however, is not necessarily a solitary activity. In psychoanalytic writing, there is often a reader in mind as one proceeds. The fantasy of how the reader will react to a turn of phrase or a radical new perspective on theory or technique shapes and influences what appears on the page. Yet much of the creative process develops in isolation as one thinks about the kernel of an idea over and over in different settings. This contemplative period may take days, weeks, or even years.

104

Most writing involves some oscillation between, on the one hand, quiet reflection on what one has to say, and, on the other, imagined responses by potential readers. An imaginary audience is a fixture in Freud's writing. Time and again, he invents an imaginary skeptical audience, masterfully anticipates the objections of that audience/reader to his argument, and offers a compelling rebuttal.

When the text is co-authored, further complexity is introduced into the process. In addition to the solitary contemplation and the imagined interaction with a reader, a collaboration with another writer requires a special sensitivity to one's co-author—after all, each sentence must represent two authors, not one.

One such example of collaboration emerged in the course of writing this chapter. We began with a shared idea—namely, an updating of Freud's 1914 idea that what is definitive of analysis as a treatment for psychological problems is the grounding of the work in the understanding of transference and resistance. We planned to describe how our own definition of analysis has evolved from and/or is discontinuous with Freud's 1914 ideas. We began our work on this collaborative project with enthusiasm. However, we found that the words did not flow as freely as we had hoped from either of us.

Feeling stuck in our efforts to get things moving, we reread and studied Freud's 1914 text. We were singularly disappointed as we came to recognize that much of Freud's paper was a rather vitriolic polemic against Jung's departures from Freud's theoretical premises and a fierce insistence that he and he alone was the founder of psychoanalysis. Hence, we came to understand that the defensiveness in Freud's tone was a reflection of his insecurities regarding competing claims of authorship of his idea (i.e., of psychoanalysis as a discipline) and a fear that Jung would subvert what he had invented and continue to call it "psychoanalysis". We had picked a quotation that caught Freud at an inauspicious moment in the history of his own psychological maturation.

As our enthusiasm waned, we had to rethink the theme of our chapter. We traded revisions back and forth until we began to clarify that what was most pressing to us was not the task of proposing a contemporary definition of psychoanalysis. Rather, the collaboration itself had served to clarify for each of us how we had evolved as analysts over thirty years of practice. We talked at length with one another about how each of us had come to his current, evolving sense of himself as a psychoanalyst. Our developmental experiences in the course of analytic training and in the early years afterwards were markedly different in some respects, and yet we found that there was great overlap in how we conceived of the way we work and who we are as psychoanalysts. Although we have known one another for more than twenty years, we found that we came to know each other in a new way in the course of these discussions. But with regard to the task of deciding what we hoped to achieve in co-authoring a chapter, talking alone was not sufficient. Only by our repeated efforts to write our thoughts (or, more accurately, to allow ourselves to see what we thought in the very act of writing) were we eventually able to discern what it was that we wanted to attempt. Putting words to the page forced us (and freed us) to transform inchoate thoughts and feelings into concepts and an idea of what it was that we wanted to communicate in the form of a co-authored analytic chapter.

In thinking about how readers might respond to our perspective, we recognized that our maturational experiences might not be shared by other analysts. We certainly did not want to be prescriptive in our tone. We thus made a concerted effort to present our ideas as simply a description of our own experiences, rather than suggesting that they are universal. We became clearer with ourselves that among the qualities of an analyst that we view as most important is the way in which an analyst makes use of what is unique and idiosyncratic to his or her personality.

Working with a co-author also involves an experience of having a built-in editor or consultant (whether or not one wants one) who can offer an "outside" perspective on the other author's clinical material. In the course of our collaboration on this chapter, one of us (T.H.O.) sent a draft of it to his co-author containing the clinical vignette presented above involving the earthquake dream. The co-author (G.O.G.) responded (in written form) with the following thoughts about the case in general and the dream in particular:

> I very much agree with your point that the dream cannot be ascribed to the patient alone, but to a co-constructed subject. I felt that the dream was as much yours as his. My fantasy about the dream is this: that even though you had perceived your analyst as treating you in a generic manner, you felt some sort of protection—a safe harbor, if you will—in resorting to his style of speaking. In doing so, you had not separated from him and thus did not have to bear the pain associated with the loss of him. I am reminded of Freud's famous comment that the only way the ego

can give up an object is to take it within. The earthquake, then, could be seen as a growing awareness in the patient that you were about to be ripped from your internally created house—i.e., the safe harbor of your analyst's office or internalized presence—and cast into a world where you must speak in your own voice. At some level, the patient felt that way about being ripped from his father's "house." What was going on in you had a great deal of resonance with what was going on in him. I did not add this to the paper—because it is purely my own conjecture and may not fit with your experience.

As this quotation indicates, a co-author's perspective on clinical material must then be filtered through the thoughts of the author providing the clinical data in order to see if it is "a good fit" with the actual analytic moment described. Ogden, who was not used to such "interference" with his writing process, found himself feeling unsettled by Gabbard's unexpected comments. He required more than two months of "sleeping on" (dreaming) what had been elicited in him by Gabbard's note before he was able to offer a considered response (also in written form):

On rereading my account of my work with Mr. A, I find it telling that I saw in the invariability of the photograph in the patient's dream only stasis, as opposed to reliability; and that I saw in the absence of the photographer in the photograph only the absence of a thinking/feeling person, as opposed to unobtrusiveness. Your comments on the vignette helped me to see what had been there all along in my writing of the account: my deep appreciation of what I feel to be two of my first analyst's best qualities—his willingness to remain emotionally present during trying times in the analysis and during very difficult times in his life, and his ability to "stay out of the way" (and not reflexively make transference interpretations) when I was doing psychological work on my own in the sessions.

The co-authors view the emotional experience that Ogden describes as a current response both to his memory of his work with Mr. A and to Gabbard's comments on his written account of that experience. This exchange between the co-authors constitutes a type of maturational experience that was of value to both authors.

Daring to improvise

With each patient, we have the responsibility to become an analyst whom we have never been before. This requires that we drop the script and enter into a conversation, a conversation of a type we have never before experienced (Hoffman, 1998; Ringstrom, 2001). This may take the form of responding to a patient's mention of a film by saying, "There's hardly a word spoken in the entire film, at least that's how it left me feeling." With another patient, improvising may mean remaining silent, not complying with implicit coercive demands for reassurance or even for the sound of the analyst's voice. Improvisation is, of course, a theatrical metaphor. The great Russian acting teacher Constantin Stanislavski once noted, "The very best that can happen is to have the actor completely carried away by the play. Then regardless of his own will he lives the part, not noticing how he feels, not thinking about what he does, and it all moves of its own accord subconsciously and intuitively" (1936, p. 13). In an analogous way, maturation as an analyst involves increasingly allowing ourselves to be caught up in the moment (in the unconscious of the analysis) and carried by the music of the session. Analysis is not an experience that can be mapped out and planned. Events happen between two people in a room together, and the meaning of those events is discussed and understood. Analysts learn more about who they are by participating in the "dance" of the moment. The extent to which the analysis is "alive" may depend on the analyst's willingness and ability to improvise, and to be improvised by, the unconscious of the analytic relationship.

The analyst's unconscious effort to disturb his own psychic equilibrium

What at one time might have been called being reliable, stable, and trustworthy may gradually become too easy and more than a little stale and predictable. We at times become aware during a session with a patient that we have become too comfortable with ourselves as analysts. "Errors," in these sessions, can often be seen as expressions of the healthiest parts of ourselves and are invaluable to our maturation if we can make use of these alerts. Such "errors" include the analyst's arriving late for a session, ending a session early, falling asleep during a session, and expecting a different patient when the analysand in the waiting room. (Not included in this type of error are boundary violations such as having sex with patients, breaches of confidentiality, entering into a business relationship with a patient, and so on [Gabbard and Lester, 1995].) The errors that do not involve boundary violations very often represent the analyst's unconscious efforts to disturb his own psychic equilibrium, to force himself to take notice of the ways in which he has become stagnant in his role as analyst.

We believe that there is a self-imposed need to be original—not in the sense of a narcissistic display, but in the sense of a need to quietly, steadily, unselfconsciously enter into conversation with the patient or supervisee in a way that could happen between no two other people in the world (Ogden, 2004a). If this is forced, it quickly reveals itself to be an empty contrivance. The development of an "analytic style" (Ogden, 2007, p. 1185) that is experienced as fully authentic is part of an ongoing effort on the part of every analyst to become an analyst in his or her own right. One can achieve this sense of having become "original" only through a painstaking effort to shed, over time, the shackles of orthodoxy, tradition, and one's own unconscious irrational prohibitions (Gabbard, 2007). The analyst's struggle with theory as master or servant may be an integral part of this effort. We share the view of Sandler (2003) that each analyst develops a private amalgam or mixed model, borrowing from certain aspects of various theories that are consistent with the analyst's own subjectivity and own approach to analysis. At the same time the analyst's we concur with Bion's notion that the analyst must endeavor to forget what he thinks he knows or knows "too well" in order to be able to learn from his current experience with the patient. Bion (1987) once said to a presenter, "I would [rely on theory only] . . . if I were tired and had no idea what was going on . . ." (p. 58).

Keeping one's eyes open to the way one is maturing/growing old

As one ages, one is able to speak from experience in a way that one could not have done previously. Often one becomes aware after the fact, that one has changed—for example, through listening to oneself speak to one's patient. Optimally, the analyst engages in a mourning process in which the loss of youth and the inevitability of old age and death are recognized, accepted, and even embraced as a new form of coming into being as a person leading an examined life. The analyst may, in this way achieve a greater appreciation for the patient's experiences of loss and the ways in which he has handled or evaded them.

This maturational process occurs both within and outside of the analytic setting. The analyst who shows up each day in the consulting room is (ideally) never entirely the same analyst who showed up the previous day. An analyst's capacity to fully grasp a patient's grief may be limited until the analyst himself has navigated his own grief associated with the loss of loved ones and the endings of important periods of his life—for example, the era in which his children are living at home or the era in which his parents are alive.

Difficulties in becoming an analyst

The reasons why an analyst may fear "growing up" as an analyst, and the ways in which he may defend himself against such fears, are legion. In this chapter, we cannot list, much less explore, these fears and defenses. In the following paragraph, we will offer a few examples of the analyst's flight from potential maturational experiences and forms of defense against such experiences.

The analyst may be afraid that he is so insubstantial as a person that it is not possible to develop a voice of his own, or be frightened of the isolation that he imagines will come with his becoming an analyst in his own terms, or fear that with a mature recognition of uncertainty will come unbearable confusion. An analyst may defend himself against these fears and others by engaging in adolescent rebellion against "the analytic establishment" in an effort to avoid defining himself in his own terms; or by speaking early on with a contrived voice of experience when, in fact, he feels painfully lacking as a consequence of his inexperience; or by embracing false certainty in the form of an intense identification with a given school of psychoanalysis, with his own analyst, with an idealized analytic writer; and so on. Finally, we must remember that as much as we love analysis, a part of us hates it as well (Steiner, 2000). Dedication to ongoing analytic work (on ourselves and with patients) consigns us not only to uncertainty, but also to facing what we least like about ourselves and others.

Concluding comments

In this chapter, we have discussed some of our maturational experiences and viewed them from several theoretical perspectives. Some readers will recognize something of their own experiences of maturing as analysts in what we have described, while others will not. Indeed, a recurring theme in our chapter has been that speaking in generic terms to patients, colleagues, and students is anti-analytic (in the sense of representing a failure to think and speak for oneself). As Bion (1987) notes in the comment cited at the beginning of this chapter, part of becoming an analyst is to evolve in a direction that is neither bound by theory nor driven exclusively by identification with others: "The analyst you become is you and you alone—that is what you use. . ." (p. 15). Analytic discourse involves what is unique, idiosyncratic, and alive in the particular experience of a given individual: Becoming an analyst necessarily involves creating a highly personal identity that is unlike that of any other analyst.

We cannot overstate the difficulty of attempting to live by this ideal. The conscious and unconscious ties that we have to what we think we know are powerful. But the struggle to overcome these ties (at least to a significant degree) is what we ask of ourselves in each session. It has been our experience that when the analyst is off balance, he does his best analytic work.

References

Bion, W. R. (1962a). Learning from experience. In *Seven servants*. New York: Aronson, 1977.

Bion, W. R. (1962b). A theory of thinking. In *Second thoughts* (pp. 110–119). New York: Aronson, 1967.

Bion, W. R. (1970). Attention and interpretation. In *Seven servants*. New York: Aronson, 1977.

Bion, W. R. (1987). Clinical seminars. In F. Bion (ed.) *Clinical seminars and other works* (pp. 1–240). London: Karnac.

Freud, S. (1914). On the history of the psychoanalytic movement. *S. E.*, 14, 1–66.

Freud, S. (1937). Analysis terminable and interminable. In *S. E.*, 23, 209–253.

Gabbard, G. O. (2000). On gratitude and gratification. *Journal of the American Psychoanalytic Association*, 48, 697–716.

Gabbard, G. O. (2003). Miscarriages of psychoanalytic treatment with the suicidal patient. *International Journal of Psychoanalysis*, 84, 249–261.

Gabbard, G. O. (2007). "Bound in a nutshell": Thoughts on complexity, reductionism and "infinite space." *International Journal of Psychoanalysis*, 88, 559–574.

Gabbard, G. O. and Lester, E. P. (1995). *Boundaries and boundary violations in psychoanalysis*. Washington, DC: American Psychiatric Publishing.

Hoffman, I. (1998). *Ritual and spontaneity in the psychoanalytic process: A dialectical constructivist view*. Hillsdale, NJ: The Analytic Press.

Loewald, H. (1960). On the therapeutic action of psychoanalysis. In *Papers on psychoanalysis* (pp. 221–256). New Haven, CT: Yale University Press, 1980.

Loewald, H. (1979). The waning of the Oedipus complex. In *Papers on psychoanalysis* (pp. 384–404). New Haven, CT: Yale University Press, 1980.

Ogden, T. H. (1991). Some theoretical comments on personal isolation. *Psychoanalytic Dialogues*, 1, 377–390.

Ogden, T. H. (1994). The analytic third: Working with intersubjective clinical facts. *International Journal of Psychoanalysis*, 75, 3–20.

Ogden, T. H. (1997). Reverie and interpretation. *Psychoanalytic Quarterly*, 66, 567–595.

Ogden, T. H. (2004a). This art of psychoanalysis: Dreaming undreamt dreams and interrupted cries. *International Journal of Psychoanalysis*, 85, 857–877.

Ogden, T. H. (2004b). On holding and containing, being and dreaming. *International Journal of Psychoanalysis*, 85, 1349–1364.

Ogden, T. H. (2005). On psychoanalytic writing. *International Journal of Psychoanalysis*, 86, 15–29.

Ogden, T. H. (2006). Reading Loewald: Oedipus reconceived. *International Journal of Psychoanalysis*, 87, 651–666.

Ogden, T. H. (2007). Elements of analytic style: Bion's clinical seminars. *International Journal of Psychoanalysis*, 88, 1185–1200.

Ringstrom, P. (2001). Cultivating the improvisational in psychoanalytic treatment. *Psychoanalytic Dialogues*, 11, 727–754.

Rosenfeld, H. (1987). *Impasse and interpretation: Therapeutic and anti-therapeutic factors in the psychoanalytic treatment of psychotic, borderline and neurotic patients*. London: Tavistock.

Sandler, J. (2003). Reflections on some relations between psychoanalytic concepts and psychoanalytic practice. *International Journal of Psychoanalysis*, 64, 35–45.

Smith, H. F. (2001). Hearing voices. *Journal of the American Psychoanalytic Association*, 49, 781–812.

Stanislavski, C. (1936). *An actor prepares* (E. R. Hapgood, Trans.). New York: Theatre Arts Books.

Steiner, J. (2000). Book review: *A mind of one's own* by R. Caper. *Journal of the American Psychoanalytic Association*, 48, 637–643.

Steiner, J. (2008). Transference to the analyst as an excluded observer. *International Journal of Psychoanalysis*, 89, 39–54.

Winnicott D. W. (1951). Transitional objects and transitional phenomena. In *Through Paediatrics to Psycho-Analysis* (pp. 229–242). New York: Basic Books, 1958.

Winnicott, D. W. (1952). Transitional objects and transitional phenomena. In *Through paediatrics to psycho-analysis* (pp. 229–242). New York: Basic Books, 1958.

Winnicott, D. W. (1958a). The theory of the parent–infant relationship. In *The maturational processes and the facilitating environment* (pp. 37–55). New York: International Universities Press, 1965.

Winnicott, D. W. (1958b). The capacity to be alone. In *The maturational processes and the facilitating environment* (pp. 29–36). New York: International Universities Press, 1965.

Winnicott, D. W. (1963). Communicating and not communicating leading to a study of certain opposites. In *The maturational processes and the facilitating environment* (pp. 179–192). New York: International Universities Press, 1965.

6

DARK IRONIES OF THE "GIFT"
OF CONSCIOUSNESS
Kafka's "A hunger artist"

Prologue

The stories of Kafka and Borges have profoundly altered the way twentieth- and early-twenty-first-century humankind thinks of itself. Very few have read their work, and yet their stories have acquired the power of myth. One need not have read or even heard a myth for the myth to exert a powerful influence on the culture in which one lives: myths are the dreams of a culture. Kafka and Borges, whose writing was part of the living pulse of the time in which they lived, committed aspects of those dreams to words and narratives. Reading their stories, novels, and poetry does not simply influence what the reader thinks; it alters the very structure of thinking, the *way* the members of a culture think. That altered way of thinking, in turn, allows the culture to dream new dreams, that is, to create new myths necessary to contain the psychological changes that the culture is in the process of making.

The stories of Kafka and Borges have spawned new words—*Kafkaesque* and *Borgesian*—to name particular qualities of human consciousness that reside primarily in the matrix, the background emotional field, as opposed to the specific symbolic content of consciousness. I use the term *consciousness* to refer to the capacity for human self-awareness; for being aware of one's awareness; for being able to experience one's thoughts, feelings, and behavior as one's own thoughts, feelings, and behavior. In the absence of consciousness, one is merely a figure in a dream/myth that is not of one's own making.

115

I have written this essay in two parts, the first, in this chapter, on Kafka and his story "A hunger artist" (1924); the second, on Borges and his fiction "The library of Babel" (1941) (see Chapter 7). In each of the two parts of this essay, I offer a biographical sketch of the author, which serves as a context for a close reading of his story.[1] I juxtapose biography and close reading not to use the text to analyse the author, or to analyse the text on the basis of inferences regarding the unconscious life of the author. Rather, it is my hope that the juxtaposition of biography and a reading of the text will generate a living conversation between the two in the mind of the reader. I will try to find words to convey aspects of my own experience of that "conversation," but, by and large, I will leave that work and that pleasure to the reader.

In an epilogue to Part II of this essay (see Chapter 7), I will compare the ways in which Kafka and Borges create, in the experience of writing and reading, the dilemmas inherent in human consciousness, as well as the ways in which characters (who reflect important aspects of the author's personality and life experience) struggle mightily in their efforts not only to face but also to do something original with those dilemmas.

Kafka

Franz Kafka led a brief, predominantly self-tormented life in which he unremittingly viewed himself as a failure at the two things that were most important to him: writing and becoming an independent adult. He elected to publish during his lifetime only a small number of his stories and none of his three unfinished novels, largely because he considered the vast majority of his work to be unworthy of

---

1 These essays and the one in Chapter 7 are the most recent in a series of papers in which I have offered close readings of the writing of psychoanalysts, creative writers, and poets. In the previous papers and in the current essay, I discuss and/or make use of the idea that, just as the meaning of language lies *in* the language, not behind it or beneath it, so, too, unconscious meaning lies in consciousness, not behind it or underneath it. See, for example, discussions of works by Frost (Ogden, 1998, 1999), Stevens (Ogden, 1997), William Carlos Williams (Ogden, 2006a), and Heaney (Ogden, 2001a); and by Freud (Ogden, 2002), Winnicott (Ogden, 2001b), Bion (Ogden, 2004, 2007b), Loewald (Ogden, 2006b), and Searles (Ogden, 2007a).

publication. With the exception of two periods, each lasting only two years, he spent his life living at home with his parents, even when he could have afforded to live on his own. Though he was three times engaged to marry, he broke off all three and never married or had children.

There are three principal sources of information concerning Kafka's intellectual and emotional life: detailed diaries that he kept between 1910 and 1923 (collected, edited, and published by Max Brod as *Diaries, 1910–1923* [Kafka, 1964]); more than a thousand letters that he wrote to friends and publishers; and a biography written by his closest friend, Max Brod (1960).

Kafka, the eldest of six children, was born in 1883 to a relatively wealthy, middle-class Jewish family in Prague. His two younger brothers died at the ages of one and a half years and two and a half years. It is difficult to imagine that Kafka's mother and Kafka were not profoundly affected by the deaths of two of her three small children in the space of a year (at which time Kafka was about four years old). In the years following these deaths, Kafka's three sisters were born (six, seven, and nine years after Kafka's birth).

Kafka was haunted by his father. For his entire life, Kafka felt a complex mixture of awe, fear, hatred, and genuine admiration for him. At the age of thirty-six, in a forty-five-page letter to his father (which he never sent to him), he wrote:

> You . . . [are a real Kafka] with your strength, health, appetite, decision, eloquence, self-satisfaction, superiority over the world, endurance, presence of mind, knowledge of the world, a certain largeness, and naturally [you also have] . . . all the weaknesses and failings that go with these qualities. (Brod, 1960, p. 19)

By comparison with his father, Kafka felt cowardly, ugly, and unmanly:

> I . . . was afraid of mirrors because they showed in me an ugliness which in my opinion was inevitable . . . [but] which . . . could not have been an entirely truthful reflection, for had I actually looked like that, I certainly would have attracted even more attention. (*Diaries*, January 2, 1912, pp. 159–160)

Kafka's childhood was "indescribably lonely" (Brod, 1960, p. 9). His parents were almost entirely devoted to running his father's thriving wholesale and retail haberdashery business. Kafka wrote of his childhood, "My principle [for getting through life was] to walk, to dress, to wash, to read, above all to coop myself up at my home in a way that took the least effort, and that required the least spirit" (*Diaries*, January 2, 1912, p. 161). Kafka said and wrote very little about his mother. He saw her as living under the control of his father and as having little time for her children (Kafka, 1919).

Kafka's mother tongue was German, although he spoke and wrote adequate, but not literary, Czech. He was educated at a German private school whose students and faculty were almost entirely Jewish. Anti-Semitism was a constant force in the life of every Jew living in Prague in the last half of the nineteenth century and the first half of the twentieth (Robertson, 1987). Kafka lived a highly ambivalent relationship to his own Judaism: "What have I in common with Jews? I have hardly anything in common with myself and should stand very quietly in a corner, content that I can breathe" (*Diaries*, January 8, 1914, p. 252).

The largest problem with Judaism, for Kafka, was the fact that his father was Jewish, and consequently Kafka was both strongly drawn to it and in revolt against it. He received a classical education that seems to have been almost completely without interest to Kafka, who was a middling student (Pawel, 1984).

A major element in Kafka's life was his friendship with Max Brod, which began when they were university students and lasted until Kafka's death at forty-one. Brod describes Kafka as quiet, but engaged in his life with Brod and two other friends who called themselves "The Prague Four." He was "one of the most amusing of men I've ever met, in spite of his shyness, in spite of his quietness" (Brod, 1960, pp. 39–40). Though Brod was born with a severe curvature of the spine, his irrepressible enthusiasm for life helped buoy Kafka's spirits during most of Kafka's adult life (Robert, 1992). Brod (1960) describes Kafka as "ironically considerate towards the follies of the world, and therefore full of sad humor" (p. 67).

Kafka was powerfully drawn to writing from an early age, but kept his interest a secret until well into his years at the German University in Prague (Pawel, 1984). Only after several years of friendship with Brod, Kafka cautiously admitted to him that he wrote stories. It required a great deal of trust in Brod for Kafka to show him anything of what he wrote. Having read some of Kafka's stories, Brod was convinced that Kafka was an enormously talented writer. Brod himself was a writer of poetry, fiction, plays, and literary criticism, and was widely published even during his university years; in fact, during Kafka's lifetime, of the two men, Brod was far and away the better known and more highly regarded writer.

Brod thought so highly of Kafka's work that in a published book review, Brod closed by saying that the author of the book being reviewed was one of the outstanding German-speaking contemporary writers and deserved a place alongside the three other great writers of their era, one of whom was Kafka. Brod made this statement in print despite the fact that, at the time, Kafka had not published a single line of his writing (Pawel, 1984). With Brod's help, Kafka, at twenty-three, began to publish a handful of very brief stories in literary magazines, although he himself did not think well of the writing.

Though not the slightest bit interested in law, Kafka, along with Brod, decided to take training in the law in order to ensure that they would be able to earn a living. Kafka qualified as a Doctor of Jurisprudence and did the required year-long internship in the law courts of Prague. He spent almost the entirety of the remainder of his life working as an administrator at the Worker's Accident Insurance Institute, a semi-governmental agency dealing with the safety and insurance coverage of workers. Kafka was a talented, well-liked, and well-appreciated employee who earned regular promotions throughout his career (Citati, 1990). Nonetheless, he felt ceaselessly tormented by the fact that his work left him little time and energy to write: "That I, so long as I am not freed of my office, am simply lost, that is clearer to me than anything else" (*Diaries*, January 2, 1910, p. 31). And almost two years later: "While here, in the office, . . . I must rob a body capable of such happiness [while writing] of a piece of its flesh" (*Diaries*, October 3, 1911, p. 62).

Kafka, in his twenties and early thirties, continued to live at home while working at the insurance company and writing some of his best works, including "The stoker" (1913), "Metamorphosis" (1915), and the beginnings of *The trial* (written between 1914 and 1924 and posthumously published in English in 1937). In a state of mind that was characteristic of Kafka during that period of his life, he wrote:

Anxiety alternating with self-assurance at the office. . . . Great antipathy to "Metamorphosis." Unreadable ending. Imperfect almost to its very marrow. It would have turned out much better if I had not been interrupted at the time by the business trip. (*Diaries*, January 19, 1914, p. 253)

The diaries that Kafka kept between 1910 and 1923 were not mere jottings about daily events. They constitute an ingenious piece of writing that intertwines detailed sketches of real and imaginary people; obsessive self-questioning regarding, for instance, whether or not to leave his job and how he viewed Brod's Zionism; beginnings of stories; pen-and-ink drawings (he had in adolescence considered becoming a painter instead of a writer); detailed renderings of dreams (without interpretation); highly compact pieces of literary criticism; one-sentence prose poems ("Clear night on the way home; distinctly aware of what in me is mere dull apathy, so far removed from a great clarity expanding without hindrance" (*Diaries*, January 12, 1914, p. 252).

Kafka felt increasingly driven to write, but he found the act of writing to be physically and emotionally exhausting:

> My talent for portraying my dreamlike inner life has thrust all other matters into the background. . . . But the strength I can muster for that portrayal is not to be counted upon: perhaps it has already vanished forever. (*Diaries*, August 6, 1914, p. 302)

Kafka had been a frail child and, in adolescence and adulthood, developed a host of somatic difficulties (crushing headaches that lasted for days, insomnia, fatigue, abdominal pain, and extreme sensitivity to sound). Medical examinations failed to reveal a physical etiology for any of these symptoms. Kafka admitted to himself that he was a severe hypochondriac and on many occasions took week-long "treatments" at sanatoriums where he was given the latest herbal "cure."

For Kafka, equal to writing as a measure of his worth was his ability to become a man independent of his parents, to marry, and to have children. His introduction to sex came as an adolescent when his father, in a fit of contempt for what he saw as his son's lack of virility, took Kafka to a brothel. Although Kafka, in his twenties, was able to have sex with prostitutes and with working-class women much younger than himself, he was deathly afraid that he would be impotent with a mature woman whom he liked and respected (Pawel, 1984).

Between the ages of twenty-nine and thirty-four, Kafka was mired in a relationship with Felice Bauer, a Jewish woman living in Berlin, whom he met at the home of Max Brod's father. The relationship seemed to go well in its initial months when it consisted entirely of an exchange of letters. Felice repeatedly requested that they meet in person, something that Kafka feared and put off for as long as he could. When they did finally meet, they found one another only moderately interesting and physically attractive (Canetti, 1974). They both seemed to feel that the business of getting married was an important step to take at that point in their lives, and so they doggedly persisted in trying to get Kafka through his obsessional worry that the demands of marriage would kill his ability to write. Counterbalancing his fear of marrying was his fear of growing old alone (*Diaries*, 1916).

In the course of the five-year relationship with Felice Bauer, Kafka experienced almost continuous anguish about whether to marry or to break off the relationship. They became engaged twice during these years. Both times, Kafka broke the engagement after several months. Kafka described the first engagement party:

> Was tied hand and foot like a criminal. Had they sat me down in a corner bound in real chains, placed policemen in front of me, and let me look on simply like that, it could not have been worse. And that was my engagement; everybody made an effort to bring me to life, and when they couldn't, to put up with me as I was. Felice . . . of course . . . with complete justification . . . suffered the most. What was merely a passing occurrence to the others, to her was a threat [because she was the one who would have to marry Kafka]. (*Diaries*, June 6, 1914, pp. 275–276)

Here, as in so many of Kafka's diary entries and letters, it is impossible for the reader (and, I presume, for Kafka) to separate self-pity, gallows humor, and an expression of painful feelings of helplessness regarding how to get beyond (to escape) himself and his lifelong fears. In the middle of the five-year involvement with Felice Bauer, Kafka, at thirty-two, moved for the first time from his parents' home to rented rooms; he was able to write in bursts, but would lapse into severe writer's block (for up to eighteen months); his diaries were filled with endless rumination, including lists of reasons for and against the marriage.

Prior to the second engagement to Felice, in a letter to Max Brod, Kafka imagined in a self-parodying way how they would live together:

> We'll get married . . . rent two or three rooms . . . and each be responsible for our separate financial needs. Felice will go on working as before, while I . . . lie on the couch feeding on milk

and honey [that is, he would stay at home writing]. (Pawel, 1984, p. 345)

Despite (or perhaps because of) the torment that he was experiencing in relation to the prospect of marrying, during these years Kafka wrote and published several of his most famous stories and wrote a good deal of *The trial* (1937). But Kafka was convinced that writing and living in the real world (i.e., with other people) were mutually exclusive ways of being: "I must be alone a great deal. What I accomplished was only the result of being alone . . . the fear of the connexion, of passing into the other. Then I'll never be alone again" (*Diaries*, July 21, 1913, p. 225).

But he also recognized that being alone often led him to engage in seemingly endless periods of a type of thinking that went nowhere:

Hatred of active introspection. Explanations of one's soul, such as: Yesterday I was so, and for this reason; today I am so, and for this reason. It is not true, not for this reason and not for that reason, and therefore also not so and so. (*Diaries*, December 9, 1913, pp. 244–245)

During the period of the second engagement to Felice, Kafka began coughing blood, which led to his being diagnosed with tuberculosis. Far from being devastated by the diagnosis, he was practically ebullient. Brod described Kafka's state of mind in the following terms: "Kafka sees it [tuberculosis] as psychogenic, his salvation from marriage, so to speak. He calls it his final defeat. But has been sleeping well ever since. Liberated?" (Pawel, 1984, p. 360). Not only did Kafka's chronic insomnia lift after he was diagnosed with tuberculosis; his headaches were also "flushed away," according to a letter he wrote in 1917 to Felice (Pawel, 1984, p. 360). In another letter, in September, 1917, Kafka wrote: "Sometimes, it seems to me as though brain and lungs had communicated without my knowledge. 'Things just can't go on this way,' said the brain; and after five years, the lungs offered to help" (Pawel, 1984, p. 364).

Two years after Kafka broke his second engagement to Felice Bauer, he entered into an engagement to marry another woman, only to break that engagement after six months. It was at that point that he wrote the forty-five-page letter later published as *Letter to his father* (1919).

Kafka, in failing health, moved from his rented rooms into the house of his youngest sister, Ottla. They were very close and she took care of him and doted over him. Kafka continued to work at the insurance company for short periods of time between increasingly long medical leaves. At thirty-seven, Kafka engaged in what was probably his most passionate love relationship with a woman. Milena Jesenska, a 24-year-old writer and political activist, introduced herself to Kafka in a letter asking his permission to translate his work into Czech. The correspondence became highly passionate. Kafka, once again, put off a face-to-face meeting. When they eventually met, Kafka fell deeply in love with her, but she quickly understood that she would be only an imaginary woman for him, and that he would never be able to carry on a real relationship with her (Pawel, 1984). She ended the relationship, but she had become so important to him that a year later he gave her all of his diaries.

Though Kafka achieved some recognition as a writer in Prague, his reputation never spread beyond that city during his lifetime (Citati, 1990). In the final two years of his life, as the tuberculosis spread, Kafka's strength diminished and he lost weight to the point that he became a mere skeleton of a figure. A year before he died, he met a 19-year-old woman, Dora Daimant, who had grown up in Palestine and was teaching at a Jewish children's camp near the sanatorium where Kafka was living. She seemed genuinely to love him and took very good care of him, although the two had almost no money (Pawel, 1984). The wild inflation in Germany at that time had made Kafka's pension virtually worthless. He and Dora lived simply, often without gas or electricity, because they did not have the money to pay their bills. Max Brod and Kafka's sister, Ottla, sent food to them, which was all that stood between them and starvation. Surprisingly, Dora was not at all interested in literature and seemed to view Kafka's writing as a competitor for his attention.

The impossibly high standards that Kafka held for his writing led him to publish only fourteen short stories and a number of brief sketches in his lifetime. None of his three unfinished novels—*The trial*, *The castle*, and *Amerika*—was published while Kafka was alive. In fact, Kafka instructed Max Brod, whom he appointed his literary executor, to burn all the manuscripts, notepads, drawings, letters, and diaries that were left in his apartment in Prague after his death, and to ask everyone to whom he had written letters or sent stories or diaries to return them or destroy them (Brod, 1960).

When Kafka died, Brod decided not to carry out Kafka's request. He believed that Kafka knew that Brod could never bring himself to destroy any of Kafka's letters, diaries, or manuscripts. In fact, he had told Kafka years earlier, "If you ever seriously think of [asking me to destroy your manuscripts after your death], . . . let me tell you now that I would not fulfill any such request" (Brod, 1953, p. 254). (The manuscripts that Kafka left with Dora Daimant were never published and were destroyed by the Gestapo in the late 1930s.) In addition to preserving the manuscripts, Brod devoted himself to arranging for publication of the entirety of Kafka's unpublished work, including his diaries and letters. Had Brod not made these efforts to preserve and publish Kafka's work, it is highly unlikely that Kafka would be known to us today.

The penultimate story that Kafka wrote was "A hunger artist" (1924). This was written in the spring of 1922 while Kafka was himself slowly starving to death: his tuberculosis had spread to his throat, rendering him barely able to swallow. The last piece of work that Kafka did in the final days of his life was to proofread the galleys for the publication of this story. Of all his stories, this was one of the few that he valued. In a second request to Brod, he asked that all his manuscripts be destroyed, but said that there was a handful of published works "that count" (Kafka, quoted by Brod, 1953, p. 253), one of which was "A hunger artist." But even these published stories, Kafka insisted, were not to be reprinted and, in time, "should disappear altogether" (p. 253).

Kafka's friend and doctor, Robert Klopstock, described Kafka in the last days of his life:

> Kafka's physical condition at this point and the whole situation of his literally starving to death, were truly ghastly. Reading the proofs [of "A hunger artist"] must have been not only a tremendous emotional strain but also a shattering kind of spiritual encounter with his former self, and when he had finished, the tears kept flowing for a long time. It was the first time I ever saw him overtly expressing his emotions this way. Kafka had always shown an almost superhuman self-control. (Pawel, 1984, p. 445)

On June 11, 1924, Kafka died at forty-one, a penniless, unmarried, retired administrative lawyer and little-known writer. His three sisters and Milena Jesenska were subsequently killed in German death camps. Max Brod settled in Tel Aviv, where he died at the age of eighty-four.

"A hunger artist" (1924)

Kafka's story begins:

> During these last decades the interest in professional fasting has markedly diminished. It used to pay very well to stage such great performances under one's own management, but today that is quite impossible. We live in a different world now.[2] (p. 268)[3]

In this opening sentence, a note is sounded that echoes through much of the remainder of the story: psychic time and space are contracting, time is running out, and vitality is in a state of severe decline. The second sentence has a hint of madness to it, as "professional fasting" is linked both with the grandiose phrase "great performances" and the bureaucratic fussiness of the words "quite impossible." But what is most striking about the opening of the story is the sentence: "We live in a different world now." This pronouncement creates a *we* (of narrator, hunger artist, and reader) and a *now* that have the effect of closing the door behind the reader as he enters the world of the story.

Kafka does not simply tell the reader about the world he is in the process of entering; he shows that world to the reader through the action of the language:

> At one time the whole town took a lively interest in the hunger artist; from day to day of his fast the excitement mounted; everybody wanted to see him at least once a day; there were people who bought season tickets for the last few days and sat from morning till night in front of his small barred cage; even in the

---

2 In offering close readings of a story by Kafka (1924) in Part I of this essay, and a fiction by Borges (1941) in Part II (see Chapter 7), I have elected to use English translations (by W. Muir and E. Muir and by J. Irby, respectively), as these translations are widely considered to be among the truest to the original texts. Of course, the meanings and sounds of words, and the rhythms of phrases and sentences, are different in English from those of the original German and Spanish. Nonetheless, in the readings that I will provide, I will use these English translations as texts in their own right; it is beyond the scope of this essay to provide comparisons of the translations and the original texts.

3 All page references in this section, unless otherwise specified, are to Kafka's "A hunger artist" (1924).

night time, there were visiting hours, when the whole effect was heightened by torch flares; on fine days the cage was set out in the open air, and then it was the children's special treat to see the hunger artist; for their elders he was often just a joke that happened to be in fashion, but the children stood open mouthed, holding each other's hands for greater security, marveling at him as he sat there pallid in black tights, with his ribs sticking out so prominently, not even on a seat but down among the straw on the ground, sometimes giving a courteous nod, answering questions with a constrained smile, or perhaps stretching an arm through the bars so that one might feel how thin it was, and then again withdrawing deep into himself, paying no attention to anyone or anything, not even to the all-important striking of the clock that was the only piece of furniture in his cage, but merely staring into vacancy with half-shut eyes, now and then taking a sip from a tiny glass of water to moisten his lips. (p. 268)

The entirety of an internal world is on display in this single sprawling sentence, which moves seamlessly from clause to clause. The passage is a Breughel-like collection of repellent, detailed miniatures. The effect created is that of imprisonment in a continuous, unrelenting present. The phrases are simple, composed mostly of words of one or two syllables: "small barred cage," "just a joke," "down among the straw," "ribs sticking out," "courteous nod," "constrained smile," "merely staring into vacancy." The horrific is ordinary and the ordinary is horrific. Moreover, while the story is told by the narrator in the past tense—as he presents his memories of the hunger artist —the pounding repetition of present participles further contributes to the transformation of time into an eternal present: "sticking," "giving," "answering," "stretching," "withdrawing," "paying," "striking," "taking."

The narrator and the hunger artist are closely tied, perhaps two aspects of a single person. The narrator is intimately familiar with the hunger artist's circumstances, behavior, and state of mind, and has words at his disposal, while the hunger artist is either mute or uses words (not quoted) as part of the performance. And yet it is not clear that the narrator is any more able to think than is the hunger artist. The narrator uses words to describe, but does so in a mechanical sort of way that is almost entirely devoid of feeling, self-observation, or insight into the hunger artist's or his own inner life. The hunger artist is less a person than he is a driven "creature" (p. 271). He is not given a name and, in the title of the story, he is not even "The hunger artist," he is merely "A hunger artist." Not only is he not given a name; the substitute name that he is given—*hunger artist*—constitutes a bitterly ironic misnaming, in that there is no art (i.e., creative expression of a personal aesthetic) in marathon fasting.

If his fasts are not viewed by his audience as credible, that is, genuine feats of self-starvation, the hunger artist is no one. Consequently, nothing is more important to him than demonstrating beyond doubt that he is a genuine hunger artist and not a trickster. He welcomes the closest scrutiny of his fasts:

> Besides casual onlookers there were also relays of permanent watchers . . . to watch the hunger artist day and night, three of them at a time, in case he should have some secret recourse to nourishment. . . . [Some watchers] were very lax in carrying out their duties . . . intending to give the hunger artist the chance of a little refreshment. . . . Nothing annoyed the artist more than such watchers; they made him miserable; they made his fast seem unendurable; sometimes he mastered his feebleness sufficiently to sing during their watch for as long as he could keep going, to show them how unjust their suspicions were. But that was of little use; they only wondered at his cleverness in being able to fill his mouth even while singing. (pp. 268–269)

The hunger artist's fear of being seen as a fraud is reminiscent of Kafka's incessant self-doubt regarding his capacities as a writer and as a man. The extremes to which the hunger artist goes in defending the truth of his "art" are at once impressive in their ingenuity and sadly pathetic in their blindness to the fact that his efforts are so evidently doomed to failure.

The hunger artist methodically goes about his business, but is completely unable to take any distance from it, to think about it, to learn from it:

> He was quite happy at the prospect of spending a sleepless night with . . . watchers [who took their jobs seriously]; he was ready to exchange jokes with them, to tell them stories out of his nomadic life, anything at all to keep them awake and demonstrate to them again that he had no eatables in his cage and that he was fasting as not one of them could fast. (p. 269)

The language of this sentence, to my ear, combines a reference to *Don Quixote* ("stories out of his nomadic life") that serves to underscore (by contrast) the complete absence of charm, innocence, or humor in the character of the hunger artist. In place of the naive faith of Don Quixote is the desperate obsession of the hunger artist. Moreover, the appended clause "that he was fasting as not one of them could" stands out because it affords a first glimpse into the grandiosity of the hunger artist: he feels superior to those who are unable to fast as long as he can.

Since no single person can monitor the hunger artist twenty-four hours a day for the full forty days of his performance, the hunger artist himself is therefore "bound to be the sole completely satisfied spectator of his own fast" (p. 270). In other words, the proof of the hunger artist's worth is impossible to demonstrate to anyone but himself, and yet proving his worth to himself is also impossible, as reflected by the fact that he is driven to repeat his performance again and again. He can know the verity of his fasting, but he has no ability to know the truth of who he is.

That the hunger artist's bizarre existence (his living in isolation from others and himself) is self-created makes it all the more horrific and inescapable. The hunger artist's (and Kafka's) imprisonment are complete and inescapable because the universe has shrunk to the size of the tiny cage in which they both spend their lives.

The story at this point takes an entirely unexpected turn. The narrator observes that it is not the difficulty of convincing the public of the authenticity of his fast that most troubles the hunger artist. What is far more difficult for him to bear is a fact that "he alone knew: how easy it was to fast" (p. 270). The forty-day fasts that would bring the hunger artist "to such skeleton thinness" (p. 270) are not at all difficult for the hunger artist to achieve. What is difficult for him is living with this awareness. This recognition that fasting is easy for him is the first indication that the hunger artist is capable of thinking and of self-awareness.

At this moment in the story, the hunger artist begins to become human in the mind of the reader (and, it seems, in his own mind). It is in the very act of telling the story that the narrator (who is barely distinguishable psychically from the hunger artist) achieves a form of consciousness that he has not previously been capable of. But the experience of becoming human in this way is momentary and unbearable for the hunger artist. Directly on the heels of his act of self-awareness and nascent self-recognition, the hunger artist (and the narrator) descend, once again, into mindlessness, this time in the form of bitterness and outrage. The sentence immediately following the revelation of his awareness that fasting is easy for him is the bold assertion: "It was the easiest thing in the world" (p. 270).

The language here is startling. Though not the spoken (i.e., quoted) words of the hunger artist, the reader can hear in the words "It was the easiest thing in the world" something of the boasting, taunting, arrogant voice of the hunger artist himself. The narrator is much too formal and dispassionate a character to use the vernacular in which this sentence is "spoken." The dawning self-awareness of the previous sentence is shattered by this arrogant claim. The reader can feel the hunger artist again losing himself in his all-consuming obsession. The hunger artist deplores the fact that:

> The longest period of fasting was fixed by his impresario [his manager and fellow actor in "the performance"] at forty days. . . . Why should he be cheated of the fame he would get for fasting longer, for being not only the record hunger artist of all time, which presumably he was already, but for beating his own record by a performance beyond human imagination, since he felt that there were no limits to his capacity for fasting? (pp. 270–271)

It seems that the hunger artist's awareness that fasting is easy for him renders his life pointless and futile; this self-understanding is unbearable, sending him into insane fits of outrage. Why should he endlessly demonstrate something (in the forty-day fasting performances) that is not worth demonstrating even once? The hunger artist seeks relief from this psychic pain by convulsively throwing himself into a state of crazed omnipotence, in which he proclaims that he can fast for longer and longer periods of time with each performance, and ultimately can fast with "no limits" (p. 271)—i.e., forever.

In other words, the hunger artist, unable to tolerate his moment of self-awareness, is "reduced to omnipotence" (Bion, quoted by Grotstein, personal communication, 2003). In response to momentary, unbearable self-recognition, he denies his membership in the human race—a species that requires food to live—and instead claims a place in a nonhuman world (a world "beyond human imagination" [p. 271]) that he governs by means of omnipotent thinking.

The hunger artist's descent into the imploding psychic space of omnipotence is mirrored by the declining popularity of fasting performances in Europe. For the hunger artist, this means the collapse of the external support for his madness. The narrator's descriptions of the hunger artist's physical and emotional state become even more horrifying than they have been to this point. At the end of one of the last forty-day fasting performances:

> . . . his head lolled on his breast as if it had landed there by chance; his body was hollowed out; his legs in a spasm of self-preservation clung close to each other at the knees, yet scraped on the ground as if it were not really solid ground, as if they were only trying to find solid ground. (p. 271)

The repetition, three times, of the words "as if" underscores the way in which the hunger artist is at this point "not really" a person, but only a "spasm of self-preservation" that superficially resembles a human life. The hunger artist's emergent awareness (consciousness) that fasting is easy for him has rendered his fasting performances and his very existence pointless. Self-awareness is intolerable; consciousness itself has been destroyed and replaced by omnipotent thinking. In such a state, nothing feels real or substantial (including oneself): "The ground [for him was] . . . not really solid ground." Instead, his feet scraped the ground "as if they were only trying to find solid ground," trying in vain to experience the ground as real, that is, as a solid, palpable world that has an existence outside of his mind. The hunger artist feels contempt for, and alienated from, all other people because they fail to understand what he alone knows. "To fight against . . . a whole world of non-understanding [other people's disbelief in his capacity for ever-greater feats of fasting] was impossible" (p. 273).

Once the fasting performances have gone completely out of fashion, the hunger artist joins a circus, where he occupies a cage among the animals. As time passes, people walk by his cage without giving him so much as a glance:

> He might fast as much as he could, and he did so. . . . The little notice board telling the number of fast days achieved, which at first was changed carefully every day, had long stayed at the same figure . . . and so the artist simply fasted on and on, as he had once dreamed of doing, and it was no trouble to him, just as he had always foretold, but no one counted the days, no one, not even the artist himself, knew what records he was already breaking. (pp. 276–277)

The hunger artist is now completely immersed in the world of the abject: nothing holds significance. What once completely consumed him—the quest to demonstrate to the world his capacity for longer and longer fasting performances—no longer serves to connect him to the external world. Even the number system becomes drained of meaning: forty days, sixty days, eighty days all have become indistinguishable from one another. The hunger artist is at this point floating in timelessness and meaninglessness.

Eventually, the circus overseer notices the seemingly empty cage, and discovers the weak and emaciated hunger artist buried deep in the straw at the bottom of the cage:

> "Are you still fasting?" asked the overseer, "when on earth do you mean to stop?" "Forgive me, everybody," whispered the hunger artist; only the overseer, who had his ear to the bars, understood him. . . ."I always wanted you to admire my fasting," said the hunger artist. "We do admire it," said the overseer, affably. "But you shouldn't admire it," said the hunger artist. "Well then we don't admire it," said the overseer, "but why shouldn't we admire it?" "Because I have to fast, I can't help it," said the hunger artist. "What a fellow you are," said the overseer, "and why can't you help it?" "Because," said the hunger artist, lifting his head a little and speaking, with his lips pursed, as if for a kiss, right into the overseer's ear, so that no syllable might be lost, "because I couldn't find the food I liked. If I had found it, believe me, I should have made no fuss and stuffed myself like you or anyone else." These were his last words, but in his dimming eyes remained the firm though no longer proud persuasion that he was still continuing to fast. (pp. 276–277)

This ending of the story, in its penultimate paragraph, is, for me, each time I read it, utterly a surprise. For the first time in the story, the hunger artist speaks for himself (i.e., in the form of direct quotation of his words). Also, for the first time, another character is introduced—the overseer, who is a thinking, feeling, observing person—a person who recognizes the hunger artist as a human being (as opposed to a performer or a creature) and feels genuine compassion for him.

The overseer seems to be able to "see" the infantile psychological needs of the hunger artist and is not repelled by them. This compassion is poignantly conveyed by the overseer's ordinary but profoundly tender words: "What a fellow you are." The overseer's human understanding is a necessary context for the development of the hunger artist's capacity to become self-aware, and to entrust his self-understanding to another person. The hunger artist recognizes that there is nothing admirable, and certainly nothing magical or superhuman, about his fasting: "I have to fast, I can't help it." He explains (in what I find to be the most powerful sentence of the story) why he cannot help fasting:

> "Because," said the hunger artist, lifting his head a little and speaking, with his lips pursed, as if for a kiss, right into the overseer's ear, so that no syllable might be lost, "because I couldn't find the food I liked." (p. 277)

The hunger artist's self-understanding is conveyed not only by the meanings of the words, but also by the very structure of the sentence. The words spoken by the hunger artist are literally wrapped around the tender words of the narrator. The hunger artist and the narrator, together now for the first time, feel like facets of an integrated, self-observing person who is capable of at once experiencing (being self-aware *in* the experience) and of thinking and speaking *about* the experience. After the word *because* (spoken by the hunger artist), the narrating self speaks, and in so doing, attends to—the hunger-artist-as-infant in the arms of the overseer-as-mother.

The narrator's words are delivered in seven small pieces: "Lifting his head a little/and speaking/with his lips pursed/as if for a kiss/ right into the overseer's ear/so that no syllable/might be lost." This careful portioning out of the words, to my ear, elicits the feeling of a mother feeding a baby in small spoonfuls, waiting after each portion for the infant to taste and feel and swallow the food, and then to ready himself for the next spoonful. Moreover, the sound and rhythm of the words "his lips pursed, as if for a kiss," when read aloud, create in the mouth and ear of the reader the sound and feel of a kiss. Consciousness, in these sentences, is as much a sensory event as it is a verbally symbolized cognitive event, as much an interpersonal event as it is an intrapsychic event.

The closing clause of this sentence—"Because I couldn't find the food I liked"—completes, structurally, the wrapping of the hunger artist's words around the tender words of the narrator (now the narrating/observing self). The self-awareness conveyed in this last part of the sentence is remarkable and fully unexpected. A complex sense of "I-ness" is conveyed in, and created by, the layered self-understanding that can be heard in these words. The hunger artist has desisted from eating not as a consequence of the conquest of the body by the mind, but as a consequence of the fact that he has no appetite for the food he has found to this point in his life. What is suggested—and only suggested—is the hunger artist's emerging awareness of far sadder truths: he did not find the food he liked because such food does not exist, or perhaps—even worse, because he had no appetite for any food, for any person, for life itself. One cannot help but think of Kafka, throughout his life, feeling haunted by these unspoken possibilities.

And at the same time, quietly, unobtrusively, quite a different emotional experience is being created in these same sentences: even as the hunger artist recognizes and says to the overseer that he has never found the food he liked, the reader can hear and feel in the language that the hunger artist is, in fact, drinking up that very food that he says he has never found—the "food" consisting of the feeling of loving and being loved, the experience of seeing and being seen (by the "overseer"). The sentences create an experience in reading in which the feeling of an appetite for life lived with other people is unmistakably present. There is in this moment at once the imminence of death and of new (never-before-experienced) life.

The intimacy of the spoken and unspoken conversation between the hunger artist and the overseer is shattered by the sentence that immediately follows: "If I had found it [the food I liked], believe me, I should have made no fuss and stuffed myself like you or anyone else" (p. 277). Each time I read these words, I find myself wincing. Something sacred is defiled by them. Gone is the delicate portioning out of phrases, the elegance of the holding function performed by the sentence structure, and the music of a kiss. Instead, there is the heavy-handed ("believe me") and the vulgar ("stuffed myself"). The overseer is reduced to the generic ("like you or anyone else"). It is as if all that preceded never occurred. These mindless, vulgar, dismissive words "were his last words, but in his dimming eyes remained the firm though no longer proud persuasion that he was still continuing to fast." He continued to fast, though no longer doing so arrogantly and omnipotently; he fasted because he believed that he had not found the food he liked.

The grim irony here is that he *had* found the food he liked in the experience of giving and receiving love, and of recognizing and being recognized. The tragedy of the hunger artist's life was not that he could not find the food he liked; rather, the tragedy lay in the fact that having found it (and found himself), he rejected it and himself (as well as the awareness of both). Why he had to savagely assault that state of mind in which he was aware of having found the food he liked—the experience of being lovingly seen and of seeing lovingly—is left undefined. Perhaps the hunger artist could not bear to recognize how little of the experience of lovingly seeing and being seen he had had in his life; or perhaps it was intolerable for him to recognize how little able he had been to recognize the love that had been there all along for him. Or maybe it is simply part of being human, of being self-aware, that some experiences—even the ones for which we most long—are "too much for the senses,—/Too crowding, too confusing/Too present to imagine" (Frost, 1942, p. 305). And so we turn away.

The story seems to end there, but a short paragraph remains:

> They buried the hunger artist, straw and all. Into the cage they put a young panther. . . . The panther was all right. The food he liked was brought him without hesitation by the attendants; he seemed not even to miss his freedom; his noble body, furnished almost to the bursting point with all that it needed, seemed to carry freedom around with it too. . . . The joy of life streamed with such ardent passion from his throat that for the onlookers it was not easy to stand the shock of it. But they braced themselves, crowded around the cage, and did not want ever to move away. (p. 277)

The panther, in his hunger for life, seems at first to be an incarnation of the hunger artist's dream of one day finding "the food he liked" and of being able to recognize it and allow it to fill him with "the joy of life." But on further reflection, the panther, though full of animal life and animal appetites, is not human and not self-aware. That he does not seem to notice his confinement to a circus cage— "he seemed not even to miss his freedom"—is a blessing not available to us as human beings who are condemned to experience the pain of knowing we are in pain unless we relinquish our sanity. To become human while remaining sane is to be alive to the distinctively human pain that is born of the "gift" of consciousness.

Concluding comments

In the first part of this two-part essay, I have discussed ways in which Kafka, both in his life and in "A hunger artist" (1924), seemed perennially mired in a struggle (that often felt doomed to failure) to achieve and sustain a state of being "awake" (self-aware) to himself, even at the cost of enormous psychic pain. The hunger artist—and, I believe, Kafka too—could not find in life what he wanted and needed.

Even more nightmarish than not having been able to find what he wanted in life was the possibility that the hunger artist lacked an appetite for life (that he was incapable of love or joy), and that it was for that reason that he could not "find," and would never find, the food, the people, or a sense of self that he liked. And at the same time, there is another experience, inseparable from the one I have just described, that is brought to life in the language of the story: the hunger artist did finally find the food he liked, but could take pleasure in it only for a moment before assaulting, though not completely destroying, both it and himself.

"A hunger artist" is not simply a story *about* the struggle to achieve self-awareness; it is a piece of literary art in which Kafka was engaged in an attempt to face himself in the act of writing the story. I imagine Kafka's experience of writing this story to have been an experience of creating a work of art that bore witness to the truth of who he was, and, further, an act of doing something with that truth that was adequate to it (Ogden, 2000). "We have art," Nietzsche wrote in 1888, "so we shall not be destroyed by the truth" (see Grimm, 1977, p. 67).[4] It seems to me that Kafka, in writing "A hunger artist," made art so that the truth to which that art gave shape and vitality would not destroy him.

Perhaps Kafka, unlike the hunger artist, was able to take genuine pleasure in the experience of writing this story and did not feel compelled to try to destroy the experience. This conjecture is supported by Kafka's second set of instructions to Max Brod, in which he asked that the manuscript of "A hunger artist" not be destroyed after his death, and by the tears that his friend and doctor saw "flowing for a long time" after Kafka finished reading the proofs of the story a few days before he died.

In Part II of this essay, in the next chapter, I will discuss Borges's life and his story "The library of Babel" (1941), and will conclude the discussion by comparing the ways in which Kafka and Borges handled in their lives—and in the life of their art—the creation of consciousness.

---

4 "Wir haben die Kunst, damit wir nicht an der Wahrheit zu Grunde gehn."

References

Borges, J. L. (1941). The library of Babel. In D. Yates and J. Irby (eds), *Labyrinths: Selected stories and other writings* (pp. 51–58). (J. Irby, Trans.). New York: New Directions, 1964.

Brod, M. (1953). Epilogue. In F. Kafka, *The trial* (pp. 252–256). (W. Muir and E. Muir, Trans.). New York: Penguin.

Brod, M. (1960). *Franz Kafka: A biography.* (G. H. Roberts and R. Winston, Trans.). New York: Da Capo, 1995.

Canetti, E. (1974). *Kafka's other trial: The letters to Felice.* New York: Schocken Books.

Citati, P. (1990). *Kafka.* (R. Rosenthal, Trans.). New York: Knopf.

Frost, R. (1942). Carpe diem. In R. Poirier and M. Richardson (eds), *Robert Frost: Collected poems, prose and plays* (p. 305). New York: Library of America, 1995.

Grimm, R. H. (1977). *Nietzsche's theory of knowledge.* Berlin/New York: Walter de Gruyter.

Kafka, F. (1913). The stoker. In N. Pasley (ed. and Trans.), *The transformation ("Metamorphosis") and other stories* (pp. 48–75). New York: Penguin, 1992.

Kafka, F. (1915). The metamorphosis. In N. Glatzer (ed.), *Franz Kafka: The complete stories* (pp. 89–139). (W. Muir and E. Muir, Trans.). New York: Schocken Books, 1971.

Kafka, F. (1919). *Letter to his father.* (E. Kaiser and E. Wilkins, Trans.). New York: Schocken Books, 1953.

Kafka, F. (1924). A hunger artist. In N. Glatzer (ed.), *Franz Kafka: The complete stories* (pp. 268–277). (W. Muir and E. Muir, Trans.). New York: Schocken Books, 1971.

Kafka, F. (1937). *The trial.* (W. Muir and E. Muir, Trans.). New York: Schocken Books.

Kafka, F. (1964). *Diaries, 1910–1923.* (M. Brod, ed.). (J. Kresh, M. Greenberg, and H. Arendt, Trans.). New York: Schocken Books.

Ogden, T. H. (1998). A question of voice in poetry and psychoanalysis. *Psychoanalytic Quarterly,* 66, 426–448.

Ogden, T. H. (1999). "The music of what happens" in poetry and psychoanalysis. *International Journal of Psychoanalysis,* 80, 979–994.

Ogden, T. H. (2000). Borges and the art of mourning. *Psychoanalytic Dialogues,* 10, 65–88.

Ogden, T. H. (2001a). An elegy, a love song and a lullaby. *Psychoanalytic Dialogues,* 11, 293–311.

Ogden, T. H. (2001b). Reading Winnicott. *Psychoanalytic Quarterly,* 70, 299–323.

Ogden, T. H. (2002). A new reading of the origins of object-relations theory. *International Journal of Psychoanalysis,* 83, 767–782.

Ogden, T. H. (2004). An introduction to the reading of Bion. *International Journal of Psychoanalysis,* 85, 285–300.

Ogden, T. H. (2006a). On teaching psychoanalysis. *International Journal of Psychoanalysis*, 87, 1069–1085.

Ogden, T. H. (2006b). Reading Loewald: Oedipus reconceived. *International Journal of Psychoanalysis*, 87, 651–666.

Ogden, T. H. (2007a). Reading Harold Searles. *International Journal of Psychoanalysis*, 88, 353–369.

Ogden, T. H. (2007b). Elements of analytic style: Bion's clinical seminars. *International Journal of Psychoanalysis*, 88, 1185–1200.

Pawel, E. (1984). *The nightmare of reason: A life of Franz Kafka*. New York: Farrar, Straus and Giroux.

Robert, M. (1992). *Franz Kafka's loneliness*. London: Faber and Faber.

Robertson, R. (1987). *Kafka: Judaism, politics and literature*. New York: Oxford University Press.

7

A LIFE OF LETTERS ENCOMPASSING EVERYTHING AND NOTHING
Borges's "Library of Babel"

Everything and nothing

In this second part of my essay, I take up the way Borges contributed to the creation of the consciousness of his time and ours, and the ways in which he attempted to handle the psychological problems attendant to that consciousness in his life and in the life of his literary work. I begin by offering a brief biographical sketch of Borges and then provide a close reading of his story "The library of Babel" (1941a). In the epilogue, I contrast the ways in which Kafka and Borges attempted to come to terms with the psychic pain as well as the delight made possible by human consciousness.

Perhaps the most fundamental of the differences between the two men in this connection lies in their relationship to their art. If Kafka's writing served to allow him to give shape and life to the disturbing emotional truths of his life while preventing those truths from destroying him, Borges's writing (and reading) were experiences in which he created and discovered emotional truths that both unsettled him and afforded him great pleasure and genuine feelings of joy. For both Kafka and Borges, a literary life is not an escape from "real life"; it is a life that is as real as any other.

As we shall see, in the terms of the literary life created by Borges— a form of literary life that no one else has ever created—understanding the problem of consciousness involves a set of emotional factors quite different from those that lay at the core of Kafka and his literary work. In what follows, I attempt to identify a set of emotional terms that are distinctive to Borges, and to create a context with which to appreciate the ways in which his work not only altered the development of Western literature, but also contributed to shaping the ways in which we are alive to ourselves as self-conscious beings.

Before moving to a discussion of Borges's life, I would like to insert a personal note. I began writing this essay knowing only that I wanted to spend some time with Kafka and Borges. The link between the two writers was unformed in my mind. Only in the course of researching this essay did I find not only that Borges was the first person to translate Kafka's stories into Spanish; in addition, I found that he published that translation (along with a preface to it) only months before he invented a new genre of short story (his *ficciones*).

Borges

As is the case for all of us, Jorge Luis Borges was born into language.[1] Borges's world of language comprised a simultaneity of English and Spanish. His paternal grandmother, Fanny Haslam, was born and raised in Staffordshire, England, and moved to Buenos Aires in her twenties, where she met and married an Argentine military officer, Francisco Borges. They had two sons, the younger of whom was Borges's father, Jorge Guillermo Borges, whose mother tongue was English.

Borges's mother came from an old, established Argentine family that for generations had produced famed military leaders. Borges was born in Buenos Aires in 1899 and his sister, Nora, was born two years later. His family lived in the home of his grandmother, Fanny Haslam, which was not unusual for young families at that time.

Borges's grandmother and his father loved English literature and took enormous pleasure in reading to Borges from the thousands of volumes in his father's library (all of which were written in English). "If I were asked to name the chief event in my life, I should say my

---

1 The principal sources upon which I have relied for the biographical sketch I am offering are: Borges's (1970) "An autobiographical essay" (written in English)—the most extensive personal statement that Borges, a very private man, made about his life; Borges's (1984a, 1984b, 2000) lectures on literature; and biographies by Monegal (1978), Williamson (2004), and Woodall (1996).

father's library. In fact, I sometimes think I have never strayed outside that library" (Borges, 1970, p. 209). Borges learned to read and write in English before he learned to read Spanish. "When later I read *Don Quixote* in the original, it sounded like a bad translation to me" (p. 209). Borges was so thoroughly bilingual as a child that only gradually did he realize that Spanish and English were different languages. He had thought that Spanish and English were two different forms of the same language, one a more literary form that he spoke and read with his father and grandmother, and the other a more everyday form that he spoke with his mother and the servants (Borges, 1970).

The divide between the worlds of Spanish and English was not simply a matter of language; it reflected a critical divide in Borges's sense of himself. The English language constituted a deep tie to Borges's father:

> My father was very intelligent and, like all intelligent men, very kind. . . . It was he who revealed the power of poetry to me—the fact that words are not only a means of communication but also magic symbols and music. (Borges, 1970, pp. 206–207)

The world of Spanish was, for Borges, the world of his mother's family, with its long and distinguished military history. Borges was frail as a child and felt entirely unworthy to claim a place as a descendant of the military heroes whose daguerreotypes, along with their swords and medals, were prominently displayed in the living room of the house in which he grew up:

> I felt ashamed, quite early, to be a bookish kind of person and not a man of action. Throughout my boyhood, I thought that to be loved would have amounted to an injustice. I did not feel I deserved any particular love, and I remember my birthdays filled me with shame, because everyone heaped gifts on me when I thought I had done nothing to deserve them—that I was a kind of fake. (Borges, 1970, pp. 208–209)

Borges adds, "After the age of thirty or so, I got over the feeling" (p. 209). But, by all accounts, he never completely got over the feeling. His sense of shame was to a considerable degree associated with his body, which he felt was repellent (Monegal, 1978).

Borges's tie to his mother was of a far more dependent sort than his tie to his father:

I inherited from my mother . . . her strong sense of friendship. . . . From the time she learned English, through my father, she has done most of her reading in that language. . . . She has always been a companion to me—especially in later years, when I went blind [at which point she read to him, took dictation and traveled with him]—and an understanding and forgiving friend. (Borges, 1970, p. 207)

In fact, with the exception of three years when he was in his sixties, during which he was briefly married, Borges lived with his mother until she died at the age of ninety-nine.

Borges was schooled at home until he was nine years old and had only his sister Nora as a companion, along with the two imaginary friends they invented. He spent most of his time reading, and began writing stories at the age of eight. At nine, he translated Oscar Wilde's "The happy prince" into Spanish. "It was published in one of the Buenos Aires dailies, *El País*. Since it was signed merely 'Jorge Borges,' people naturally assumed the translation was my father's" (Borges, 1970, p. 211).

Borges was born with a congenital eye disease—a degenerative illness that had afflicted his father and grandmother and three generations before her. Borges's vision was poor from birth and ran a course of progressive deterioration until age fifty-five, when he lost entirely his ability to read and write. Borges's father, a professor of English and psychology and an unpublished novelist, lost his sight completely in his forties. In addition to their love of one another and their shared love of literature, there was a sadness to the relationship between Borges and his father:

From the time I was a boy, when blindness came to him [Borges's father], it was tacitly understood that I had to fulfill the literary destiny that circumstances had denied my father. This was something that was taken for granted (and such things are far more important than things that are merely said). I was expected to be a writer. (Borges, 1970, p. 211)

In search of a treatment for Borges's father's blindness, the family moved to Switzerland in 1914, only to find themselves trapped there by the outbreak of World War I. Borges was at the time an adolescent and attended a private day school in Geneva, where he learned Latin, German, and French. Though he had been very unhappy in school in Buenos Aires, where "I was jeered at and bullied by most of my schoolmates" (Borges, 1970, p. 212), he found to his surprise that his classmates in Geneva were very kind to him:

> Without a word to me, my fellow schoolmates sent a petition around to the headmaster, which they had all signed. They pointed out that I had had to study all the different subjects in French, a language I also had to learn. They asked the headmaster to take this into account, and he very kindly did so. (Borges, 1970, pp. 214–215)

It is poignant that Borges, writing this at seventy-one, is still moved by this act of friendship that he did not expect, and, I suspect, had never before experienced.

In Europe, after graduating from secondary school (which was as far as he would pursue formal education), Borges devoted himself entirely to writing and became involved with the Spanish avant-garde literary movement (Woodall, 1996). After the war, his family returned to Buenos Aires, where Borges published his first book of poems, *Fervor de Buenos Aires* (1923). Looking back on that book, Borges said:

> I feel that all my subsequent writing has only developed themes first taken up there; I feel that all during my lifetime I have been rewriting that one book. (Borges, 1970, p. 225)

One can hear in this comment Borges's experience of the way that the future resides in the past and the past in the future.

Borges, for most of his life, was shy and awkward with women. With good intentions, his father introduced him to sex as an adolescent by taking him to a brothel in Geneva. Borges seems to have carried for the rest of his life the feeling of humiliation that derived from that experience (Woodall, 1996). As an adult, he fell in love with one woman after another, but these relationships were either short-lived or became a torment for him. "He had an endless stream of fiancées" (Monegal, 1978, p. 184). It seems that much of what he experienced as mutual love was a wishful invention on his part. Among the most painful of these relationships was an experience of unrequited love with the poet Norah Lange, a beautiful and glamorous woman, who was part of the inner circle of the Buenos Aires literary scene (Williamson, 2004).

By the time Borges was in his mid-thirties, he was well known among writers and intellectuals in Buenos Aires for both his poetry and his prose, including book reviews of imaginary works by imaginary authors (Woodall, 1996). In these reviews of books by imaginary authors, Borges was beginning to separate himself-as-the-reviewer from himself-as-a-literary-invention (i.e., the author of the imaginary book that he was reviewing).

The little money Borges was paid for the contributions he made to Buenos Aires newspapers and literary magazines was not enough for him to support himself. At thirty-six, still living at home, he took a job as an assistant librarian in a small branch of the Buenos Aires municipal library system, which was located in one of the rundown outskirts of the city. There was almost no work to do there, so Borges spent his days reading and writing in the library's subterranean stacks. The nine years that Borges worked at the library were the most lonely of his life: "They were nine years of solid unhappiness" (Borges, 1970, p. 241).

Borges began to lead a double life during his years at the library:

> Ironically, at the time I was a quite well-known writer—except at the library. I remember a fellow employee's once noting in an encyclopedia the name of a certain Jorge Luis Borges—a fact that set him wondering at the coincidence of our identical names and birthdates. (Borges, 1970, p. 242)

Already there were seeds of the division of Borges, the man of letters whose name appeared in an encyclopedia of authors, and Borges, the man who lived at home, working at the library and writing and reading whenever he could.

It was during his years at the library that Borges began to read Kafka's short stories and novels (in German). Enormously impressed with Kafka's writing, Borges, in 1938, wrote a number of book reviews and literary essays on Kafka's work and, as mentioned in earlier, was the first to publish a Spanish translation of Kafka's stories (Monegal, 1978, p. 312). In the preface to the translation, Borges comments: "The full enjoyment of Kafka's work . . . may precede any interpretation and does not depend on it" (quoted by Monegal, 1978, p. 312). In other words, the stories stand on their own as literary events—experiences in writing and reading—and need not be given significance by the discovery in them of a message or commentary on the state of the world, the human condition, and so on. This is certainly the way Borges wanted his own fiction to be read. Despite the fact that Borges was an avid reader of short stories: "[A]s a writer,

. . . I thought for years that the short story was beyond my powers" (Borges, 1970, p. 238).

On Christmas Eve of 1938 (the year that his father died, and only a few weeks after his translation of Kafka had been published), Borges was to introduce to his mother a woman whom he had been seeing for some time. That afternoon, while climbing the stairs of the woman's apartment, he suffered a deep gash to his forehead when his head hit the corner of a casement window that had been painted and left open to dry. Borges's poor eyesight had prevented him from seeing the window (Williamson, 2004, p. 238). The wound became infected and led to his developing septicemia, a very high fever, hallucinations, and loss of the ability to speak. He was hospitalized and surgery was performed to drain the infection. It was unclear for almost a month whether he would survive.

On regaining consciousness, Borges's deepest fear was that he had suffered brain damage that would prevent him from ever writing again. To prove to himself that he could still write, he decided to attempt to write in a literary form in which he had never previously written; "I decided I would try to write a story. The result was 'Pierre Menard, author of *Don Quixote*'" (Borges, 1970, p. 243). This story was not only a form of writing in which Borges had never before written, it was a form of writing in which *no one* had ever before written. "Pierre Menard" was the first of Borges's *ficciones*, a genre of short story that would profoundly affect not only the development of twentieth-century literature, but also the development of a new sense of the relationship between the author and the characters he invents and who invent him, and the relationship between the dreamer and the figures in the dream whom the dreamer dreams, and who dream the dreamer (Borges, 1941b).

Borges continued working at the library (where he wrote many of his best fictions) until 1945, the year Juan Perón was elected president of Argentina. Borges had strongly opposed Perón's bid for the presidency, publicly accusing him of being a Nazi (Monegal, 1978). Upon being elected, Perón promptly "promoted" Borges to the post of chicken inspector for the Buenos Aires municipal market. Borges, of course, resigned.

Borges continued to be an outspoken opponent of Perón during the decade of Perón's dictatorial rule, in which the constitution of Argentina was replaced by virtually unrestrained powers of the president. Borges's mother and sister were active in their opposition to Perón: his sister was imprisoned and his mother placed under house arrest (each for a period of a month) for participating in an anti-Perón demonstration. Borges felt ashamed of his cowardice, in comparison with his mother, for not participating in such demonstrations (Williamson, 2004).

Having lost his job at the library and as the only wage earner in the family, Borges had to find another way to make a living. To this point, he had been unable to lecture because of his intense fear of public speaking. Previously, when he had agreed to deliver a lecture, he would have a friend read the lecture while he sat at the back of the hall, feeling deeply ashamed. But necessity forced him to overcome his fear and, in a relatively short time, he became a very popular lecturer: "I traveled up and down Argentina and Uruguay, lecturing. . . . I enjoyed the work and felt that it justified me" (Borges, 1970, p. 245).

This was a considerable overstatement. In fact, it took Borges more than twenty years to overcome his fear of public speaking. He would have several strong drinks before lecturing, and afterward felt drained and hung over by the experience.

The same year that Perón took power—1945—Borges went into psychotherapy with a psychologist, Dr. Kohan-Miller, in Buenos Aires. (Psychotherapy was very little practiced in Buenos Aires at that time.) Kohan-Miller recalls that Borges had recently been rejected by a woman whom he loved and was struggling with his feelings of inadequacy with women. Borges also sought therapeutic help for his fear of public speaking and his feelings about his father (Williamson, 2004; Woodall, 1996).

The psychological strain for Borges of having to earn a living as a public lecturer was enormous. For reasons that are impossible to delineate with any certainty, during his tenure at the library and for a period of approximately a decade thereafter, he very gradually invented a persona known as "Borges." As time went on, even his closest friends called him Borges. Borges lived in a complex relationship with "Borges," a relationship he captured in one of his most poignant works, "Borges and I" (Borges, 1957):

> The other one, the one called Borges, is the one things happen to. . . . I know of Borges from the mail and see his name on a list of professors or in a biographical dictionary. . . . I live, let myself go on living, so that Borges may contrive his literature, and this literature justifies me. . . . I shall remain in Borges, not in myself

(if it is true that I am someone), but I recognize myself less in his books than in many others or in the laborious strumming of a guitar. . . . I do not know which of us has written this page. (pp. 246–247)

There is no simple relationship between Borges and "Borges"; the two are intertwined, but nonetheless "the other one" provided Borges some cover at the point in his life that he was forced onto the public stage. In an important sense, Borges in this way invented himself (and lost himself) as a character in the story that was his life: "Thus my life is a flight and I lose everything and everything belongs to oblivion, or to him [the other one]" (Borges, 1957, p. 247). Borges's life became not simply *like* literature, it became literature, and some said that he spoke literature.

This development should not be viewed as one that diminished Borges's experience of himself and his life. Literature, for Borges, both as a reader and a writer, was a source of enormous pleasure, perhaps the greatest of joys that life held for him. That joy is unmistakable as Borges (1984a) says of reading *The divine comedy*:

No one has the right to deprive himself of this pleasure. . . . It has accompanied me for so many years, and I know that as soon as I open it tomorrow I will discover things I did not see before. I know that this book will go on, beyond my waking life, and beyond ours. (p. 25)

The supreme importance to Borges of books and literature can also be heard in his comment:

I believe that books will never disappear. It is impossible that that will happen. Among the many inventions of man, the book, without a doubt, is the most astounding. (Borges, 1984b, p. 34)

And in a lighter vein: on finding a book on Norse literature in his favorite bookstore, Borges said to the owner that it was a pity that he could not buy the book because he already had it at home (Barnstone, 1993).

When Perón was overthrown by a military junta in 1955, Borges—by this time a popular and influential public figure in Argentina—was appointed director of the National Library. This was the same year that Borges's blindness progressed to the point that he could no longer read or write. He wrote (dictated) of "God's splendid irony in granting me at one time 800,000 books and darkness" (Borges, 1970, p. 250).

Borges's sixties were a highly eventful time for him. Sharing with Samuel Beckett the Fomentor Prize, an international literary award, gave Borges international recognition for the first time. Collections of his fictions as well as his books of poetry and essays, were now published in English and five other languages. He began going on international lecture tours and took visiting professorships in major universities in the United States and Europe. His mother accompanied him on most of these trips. Because of his blindness, he was no longer able to write his tightly constructed fictions or even free verse poetry.

During this period, Borges married, largely because he believed that having become completely blind, he needed help in managing his own affairs and taking care of his mother, who was then in her eighties (Williamson, 2004). Even after marrying, Borges took most of his meals with his mother. Not surprisingly, the marriage was a failure and, after three years, Borges left his wife and moved back in with his mother.

Concurrent with these events, Borges was falling in love with a woman more than thirty years his junior whom he met when she was a university student taking one of his seminars on Norse languages and mythology. María Kodama was to become the great love of Borges's life. She was a fiercely independent woman and, during the entirety of their twenty-year relationship, refused to give up earning a living of her own or to be swallowed up by Borges's fame. María's close relationship with her Japanese Buddhist father contributed greatly to the development of her thoughtfulness and independence. From childhood, she was determined never to marry. Her intelligence, which was combined with a deeply compassionate spirit, had a profound influence on Borges in the final two decades of his life.

Beginning during the years of his brief marriage, Borges began to make very serious errors in judgment. When Perón, in 1973, returned from exile and was, by a landslide, reelected president of Argentina, Borges was appalled by what he viewed as the ignorance of the Argentine electorate; at that point, he lost faith in the ability of the Argentine people to create a democracy. Three years later, Borges welcomed the military overthrow of Perón's wife, Isabelita (who had succeeded Perón as president when he died in office in 1974).

General Augusto Pinochet, who was then presiding over a reign of terror in Chile, took the opportunity to profit from Borges's political naiveté, confusion, and disillusionment. Borges, despite strong objections on the part of his friends and family, traveled to Chile several times in the 1970s as Pinochet's guest. He was presented with awards and honorary academic degrees. In 1976, Borges dismissed democracy as a "superstition" (Borges, quoted by Williamson, 2004, p. 425) and referred to the despotic military regime in Argentina as "a government of soldiers, of gentlemen, of decent people" (p. 425). Pablo Neruda, the Nobel Prize-winning Chilean poet, denounced Borges for his support of Pinochet. This was the end of any chance that Borges might have had to win a Nobel Prize.

In the face of public denunciation by Neruda and many others, Borges withdrew from public life in Argentina. His love and attention became increasingly focused on María Kodama. They were constant companions, but at the same time led independent lives. Borges asked her to marry him several times, but each time she refused. Their love was a transformative experience for Borges that affected every sector of his life.

Gradually, he gave up his ideal of the enlightened despot, and instead developed a genuine belief in democracy in Argentina. In October 1983, on the evening when the results of a democratic election in Argentina were announced, Borges said in an address to a group of writers, intellectuals, and political leaders, "I had lost faith in democracy, believing it would result in chaos. But what happened [today] on October 30 gives us the right, the duty, to be hopeful" (Williamson, 2004, pp. 466–467).

Borges and María Kodama spent much of the last years of his life in Geneva, which he considered his second home. In 1986, after being diagnosed with terminal liver cancer, he again asked María to marry him. This time she accepted. Borges died in Geneva three months later, in June 1986, and was buried there. His headstone is inscribed in one of the Norse languages that Borges and María had spent more than twenty years studying together. The inscription is a quotation from a Norse myth, a love story, in which Borges and María had often imagined themselves to be characters.

"The library of Babel" (1941a)

I will now look closely at one of Borges's richest and most haunting fictions, "The library of Babel." It is a story that Borges published in 1941 while working at the library, still living at home, and feeling terribly isolated but becoming increasingly well known in Buenos Aires as an imaginative writer.

The epigraph to "The library of Babel" reads:

By this art you may contemplate
The variation of the 23 letters . . .

The Anatomy of Melancholy, part 2,
sect. II, mem. IV (1941a, p. 51)

The words of the epigraph, a sentence fragment, look back at the reader blankly, indecipherably. The author's name is conspicuously absent. Is he or she an imaginary author of an imaginary book? Or are the book and the quoted passage so familiar to the author (or to the narrator?) of the story that he believes there is no need to state the name of the author to a reasonably educated reader?

The second possibility is more likely correct. My own research regarding the epigraph has revealed that *The anatomy of melancholy* is a real text written in 1621 by Robert Burton. Paragraph IV of the second section of Part 2 of Burton's immense book discusses the ways in which contemplating "the variation of the 23 letters" of the alphabet constitutes a critical part of the healthy "exercise of body and mind" (Burton, 1621, p. 460). The "23 letters" are those of the classical Latin alphabet (originating circa 700 B.C.), from which the present-day alphabet of most Western languages is derived. The sounds of the letters J, U, and W were produced by combinations of other letters.

What a strange, evocative way to speak of reading and writing: "the variation of the 23 letters." The epigraph has an odd cultishness to it. A few readers do not need to be told who the author is or what "the 23 letters" are. There is an unstated suggestion that readers who know Burton's text intimately are bound together as members of a secret group, unknown to the rest of us who go about our everyday lives ignorant of the Latin alphabet, of Burton's *The anatomy of melancholy*, and of the cult, bound together by their shared knowledge of such things. In short, the design of the world and society has an invisible, secret, literary structure to it.

The story, which has already begun with the epigraph, begins again in its opening paragraph:

The universe (which others call the Library) is composed of an indefinite and perhaps infinite number of hexagonal galleries, with vast air shafts between, surrounded by very low railings. From any of the hexagons one can see, interminably, the upper and lower floors. (Borges, 1941a, p. 51)[2]

The very first thing that the narrator wants the reader to know is that the world is divided between those who refer to the "indefinite and perhaps infinite number of hexagonal galleries" as "the universe" and those who call it "the Library." This schism continues the theme of the cult, now made up of those who believe the universe to be a library.

The first paragraph continues:

The distribution of the galleries is invariable. Twenty shelves [lined with books], five long shelves per side, cover all the sides except two; their height, which is the distance from floor to ceiling, scarcely exceeds that of a normal bookcase. One of the free sides leads to a narrow hallway which opens onto another gallery, identical to the first and to all the rest. To the left and right of the hallway there are two very small closets. In the first, one may sleep standing up; in the other, satisfy one's fecal necessities. Also through here passes a spiral stairway, which sinks abysmally and soars upwards to remote distances. In the hallway there is a mirror which faithfully duplicates all appearances. Men usually infer from this mirror that the Library is not infinite (if it really were, why this illusory duplication?); I prefer to dream that its polished surfaces represent and promise the infinite . . . Light is provided by some spherical fruit which bear the name of lamps. There are two, transversally placed, in each hexagon. The light that they emit is insufficient, incessant. (p. 51, ellipsis in original)

As in the epigraph, but now magnified manyfold, there is a surfeit of numbers. Paradoxically, the structure of the Library is at once precisely quantifiable—definable and measurable in terms of numbers, geometry, and symmetries—and yet it is indefinably large, formless, perhaps extending infinitely in all directions.

---

2 Unless otherwise specified, all page numbers in this section refer to "The library of Babel" (Borges, 1941a).

The narrator's voice begins to take shape immediately in the epigraph and continues to be fleshed out in the opening paragraph. There is something odd and intriguing to such phrases as "satisfy one's fecal necessities" and "I prefer to dream that its [the mirror's] polished surfaces represent and promise the infinite": the language bespeaks an idiosyncratic, expansive (perhaps insane) way of thinking and speaking.

Who is the author of this text and to whom is the writer writing? And who inserted the ellipsis (after the phrase "promise the infinite" in the passage quoted above)? What was left out? Each word, each piece of punctuation is a marker or clue. The story is not about the mysterious structures of the universe and society; it is itself a mysterious, labyrinthine, literary structure.

The final three sentences of the opening paragraph are puzzling: "Light is provided by some spherical fruit which bear the name of lamps. There are two, transversally placed, in each hexagon. The light they emit is insufficient, incessant" (p. 51). The ambiguity of these sentences raises a great many questions in the mind of the reader: Do spherical fruit cast light or is the word "lamps" being replaced by the words "spherical fruit," but continuing to mean illuminating objects? If so, words are arbitrary and can be interchanged with other words (that is, with other variations of the twenty-three letters). In this way, in the space of a single sentence, the author (Borges? the narrator?) of the text suggests that there may be a disconnection of language from the real world to which it purports to be tightly bound in its capacity to give names to objects, feelings, ideas and so on. The experience of reading these sentences is that of a combination of a feeling of extraordinary density (a density born of an immense concentration of ideas in a very few words) and a feeling of a great expanse stretching outward infinitely as words outgrow their meanings, to the point of meaning anything—and, consequently, mean nothing.

Already in this opening paragraph, the reader experiences both a sense of wonder at the feat of literary imagination that Borges is carrying off and a sense of sadness in response to the sound of the voice with which the story is being told. The author is clever—perhaps too clever, too adept at feats of imagination. The voice of the narrator is the voice of a man who has seen (imagined) something wondrous, an infinite Library, and yet that wondrous Library, even though it may be infinite, is all there is—there is no animal life, plant life, love life, sex life, landscape, theater, and so on. There are only books describing such things. And the imaginary author (and perhaps Borges, the "real author") is a prisoner in it (and in his own vast imagination). The paradox that the Library is everything (the universe) and nothing (only a collection of books) "sinks abysmally and soars upwards to remote distances."

At still another level, there is the question of where fiction stops and where an only slightly disguised autobiography starts. How does one separate Borges (the "real" man who grew up in his father's library and never left it, the man who spent nine lonely years working in the branch library) from "Borges" (the narrator-as-character in his own story)? Is the author inventing himself (not simply a metaphor for himself) in the act of writing this story? *Biography*, a word with its etymological roots in the Greek words meaning "writing life," suggests that writing not only tells the story of a life, it creates that life in the act of writing it. This was certainly true of Borges.

As the story continues, the narrator explains (to whom?) that there are two axioms concerning the Library:

> First: The Library exists *ab aeterno* . . . [and will continue for a] future eternity. . . . Second: *The orthographical symbols* [in which the books are written] *are twenty-five in number.* (pp. 52–53, italics in original)

A footnote appended to the end of the second of these sentences reads as follows:

> The original manuscript [of the piece of writing that the reader is reading, i.e., "The library of Babel"] does not contain digits or capital letters. The punctuation has been limited to the comma and the period. These two signs, the space and the twenty-two letters of the alphabet [an alphabet that is a real precursor of the classical Latin alphabet] are the twenty-five symbols considered sufficient by this unknown author. (*Editor's note.*).
>
> (p. 53, footnote 1, italics in original)

There are several startling revelations in this footnote. First, the text that we are reading is not the original text, but a transliteration of a text originally written in the twenty-two letters of a precursor to the classical Latin alphabet. So the author of the text that we are reading is not solely the original "unknown author," but also the *"Editor,"* who is the author of the footnote. Up to this point, the reader has been only dimly aware of the Editor, who, we now realize, was the author who deleted a portion of the text and left the ellipsis in place of the missing words. So the line of authorship of the text runs from the original "unknown author" (who is the narrator), to the "Editor," to the "real author" (Borges), who is creating "Borges" (the public persona) in the act of writing this story, while "Borges" (the public persona) is at the same time creating Borges (the person from whom "Borges" is inseparable).

Thus, the literary infinite is not an abstract concept in this story; it is alive as a literary event in the experience of writing and reading. (The emergence of "Borges" may have been only dimly perceived by Borges at the time he wrote this story, but in retrospect, that process adds an important dimension to the story.)

The finding "300 years ago" (p. 53) that every book in the Library is composed of seemingly random variations of the twenty-two letters of the alphabet, the period, the comma, and the space:

> ... made it possible ... to formulate a general theory of the Library and solve satisfactorily the problem which no conjecture had deciphered: the formless and chaotic nature of almost all the books. One [of these impenetrable books composed of apparently non-sensical combinations of letters and spaces] which my father saw ... was made of the letters MCV, perversely repeated from the first line to the last. ... Some insinuated that each letter could influence the following one and that the value of MCV in the third line of page 71 was not the one the same series may have in another position on another page, but this vague thesis did not prevail. Others thought of cryptographs; generally, this conjecture has been accepted, but not in the sense in which it was formulated by its originators. (pp. 53–54)

In these sentences, an imaginary scholarly theory of a book composed of three letters and a space repeated on every page is proposed, momentarily considered (in the time that it takes to pause for a comma), and then rejected: "this vague thesis did not prevail." Time in the Library is, in this way, transformed into a literary event, a product of reading a text as opposed to the product of a measurement of the movement of the earth around the sun or the disintegration of an isotope of uranium.

But a moment later (in the time that it takes to pause for a period between sentences), an alternative imaginary theory (or theory of the imaginary) is proposed: the letters of the book are cryptographs.

This theory, we learn, has been generally accepted (though we are not given the reasons for its acceptance), but "not in the sense that it was formulated by its originators" (p. 54). In other words, the interpretation of the text that was later found to be true by subsequent interpreters was not true in the sense that its original interpreters had in mind.

It seems to me that Borges is parodying literary criticism—a literary critic can find meaning in any piece of writing, even when the text is composed of three letters and a space endlessly repeated. And another literary critic can take that interpretation of the seemingly non-sensical text and create an interpretation that seems to be in accord with the first, but actually means something entirely different. By extension, a text can mean anything and consequently means nothing. (Borges is very likely also referring to the various numerical readings of the *Kaballah*, "a book impervious to contingencies, a mechanism of infinite purposes, of infallible variations, of revelations lying in wait, of superimpositions of light. . . . How could one not study it to absurdity . . .?" [Borges, 1932, p. 86].)

The two axioms of the Library—that the Library has always existed and always will exist, and that all of the books are composed of the 25 orthographical symbols:

> . . . made it possible for a librarian of genius . . . [to deduce] that the Library is total and that its shelves register all the possible combinations of the twenty-odd orthographical symbols (a number which, though extremely vast, is not infinite): in other words, all that it is given to express, in all languages. Everything: the minutely detailed history of the future, the archangels' autobiographies, the faithful catalogue of the Library, thousands and thousands of false catalogues, the demonstration of the fallacy of those catalogues, the demonstration of the fallacy of the true catalogues, the Gnostic gospel of Basilides, the commentary on that gospel, the commentary on the commentary on that gospel, the true story of your death, the translation of every book in all languages, the interpolations of every book in all books. (p. 54)

What an extraordinary way to create, in the experience of reading, a sense of all time being present in an endless present moment: all thoughts, all ideas, all feelings, everything there is to express—from the eternity of the past to the eternity of the future—is contained in the Library at every moment.

Since it was thought that "everything" is contained in the Library, it was "hoped that a clarification of humanity's basic mysteries . . . might be found" (p. 55). But these hopes waned and the number of suicides grew. Because every possible book is included in the Library, there were long periods of time (we are told by the narrator, who is now the historian of the imaginary) in which it was believed that "there was no personal or world problem whose eloquent solution did not exist in some hexagon" (p. 55). Moreover, it was hoped that each man might be able to find the book that "vindicated" (p. 55) him and his life, "but the searchers did not remember that the possibility of a man's finding his Vindication . . . can be computed as zero" (p. 55). How different this sentence would read if, instead of using the phrase "computed as zero," Borges had written "was nil." The "mathematics" of an imaginary world is invented in the space of three words—"computed as zero."

Eventually, the searchers, weary from years of travel through the endless stacks of the Library, gave up hope. "Obviously, no one [now] expects to discover anything" (p. 55). In response to the recognition that it is impossible to find that book that offers a "vindication" of one's life, maniacal sects emerge, which:

> . . . believed that it was fundamental to eliminate useless works. They invaded the hexagons, showed credentials which were not always false [this "aside" never fails to make me smile], leafed through a volume with displeasure and condemned whole shelves —their hygienic, ascetic furor caused the senseless perdition of millions of books. (p. 56)

But the damage done by these naive men was inconsequential for two reasons:

> One: the Library is so enormous that any reduction of human origin is infinitesimal. The other: every copy is unique, irreplaceable, but (since the Library is total) there are always several hundred thousand imperfect facsimiles: works which differ only in a letter or a comma. (p. 56)

The reader can hear in these sentences the collision of the infinite possibilities of the imagination and the infinitesimal significance of the mark that one man can make on the universe. And yet, at the same time, every book in the Library is unique—"*there are no two* identical books" (p. 54, italics in original)—and, by extension, each of us is "unique, irreplaceable" (p. 54), regardless of the fact that none of us is the least bit indispensable to the universe.

After several more iterations of the futility of attempting to get language to hold the meanings that one intends to communicate, the narrator sinks into alternations of nihilism and religious fervor, both of which are at once sad and ridiculous:

> I pray to the unknown gods that a man—just one, even though it were thousands of years ago!—may have examined and read it [the "total book" that contains the entirety of the truth of the Library]. If honor and wisdom and happiness are not for me, let them be for others. Let heaven exist, though my place be in hell. Let me be outraged and annihilated, but for one instant, in one being, let Your enormous Library be justified. (p. 57)

Of course, in what sounds like feverish religiosity, there is self-parody and sardonic reference to the human wish for a Father, a "Man of the Book" (p. 56) (and Borges's personal need to become a celebrated author in order to fulfill his father's literary aspirations). The existence of such a man would justify a life lived in the Library. This expansiveness dissolves into an odd nihilism (one that is crackling with irony). The narrator describes the circumstances of his present day: "I know of districts in which the young men prostrate themselves before books and kiss their pages in a barbarous manner, but they [are illiterate and] do not know how to decipher a single letter" (p. 58).

In the final paragraph of the story, the narrator rather obsessively ponders the question of how the Library can be infinite while the number of books in it is finite (limited by the finite number of combinations of the twenty-five orthographical symbols). He proposes a solution:

> *The Library is unlimited and cyclical.* If an eternal traveler were to cross it in any direction, after centuries he would see that the same volumes were repeated in the same order (which, thus repeated, would be an order: the Order). My solitude is gladdened by this elegant hope. (p. 58, italics in original)

The "solution to the ancient problem" (p. 58) of the Library—that the Library is unlimited and cyclical—is, to my mind, not at all "elegant." In fact, this idea has already been proposed early on in the story: "*The Library is a sphere whose exact center is any one of its hexagons and whose circumference is inaccessible*" (p. 52, italics in the original). This cannot possibly be lost to Borges. He attaches a footnote to the final word of the story (which makes that final word no longer the final word). The footnote reads:

> Letizia Alvarez de Toledo has observed that this vast Library is useless: rigorously speaking, a *single volume* would be sufficient, a volume . . . containing an infinite number of infinitely thin leaves . . . [of which] the inconceivable middle page would have no reverse. (p. 58, footnote 1, italics in original)

This is truly an elegant ending to the story. The narrator declares that the story we have just read is "useless." By implication, the Library is only a metaphor (a poor one at that), and the history of the Library, written in an early Latin alphabet as an edited version of "the scrawlings" of an unknown author, is all a useless invention. There is no Library, no history of the Library, no unknown author, no editor. In other words, the final footnote is written by "the real author," by Borges.

But in closing the fiction with a footnote written by "the real author" (Borges himself), the real author (Borges) is becoming a character in his own story. The fiction is in this way becoming infinite: it can expand to include within itself any "reality" thrown its way, even the reality of its author. And yet the story is not the universe—it is only a collection of markings on a page that the reader puts down after reading it. The story is *just a story*: "The world, unfortunately, is real; I, unfortunately, am Borges" (Borges, 1947, p. 234).

Epilogue: Writing as a response to the problem of consciousness

In the final section of this essay, I will briefly compare the experience of the struggle with human consciousness that is created in "A hunger artist" (Kafka, 1924) (see Chapter 6) with that created in "The library of Babel" (Borges, 1941a). I will relate elements of the lives of Kafka and Borges to the distinctive nature of consciousness that each created, brought to life in his stories, and attempted to come to terms with in the act of writing.

"A hunger artist" is a powerful, imaginative rendering of much of what Kafka found to be most painful in his life. As I have discussed, there are two points in the story when the hunger artist begins to wrench himself out of the performance that, for him, substitutes for a self-aware life in the world as a human being. In the first of these attempts, he admits to himself that fasting is easy. He recognizes that the performances are real in the sense that the fasts are authentic, but they are also lies, in the sense of the falsity of the "theater" of the pain of hunger involved in the performances of marathon fasting.

But that window of self-awareness is immediately slammed shut in the sentence that follows, as the hunger artist defiantly asserts (through the voice of the narrator) his superhuman power: "It was the easiest thing in the world" (Kafka, 1924, p. 270). In the arrogant tone of this claim, the hunger artist takes his achievement of self-awareness (his recognition of the essential misrepresentation involved in the performance) and transforms it into a self-deception (the opposite of self-awareness). The untruthfulness of the claim does not lie in its manifest level (that fasting is easy for him), but in the tone of the assertion, which lays claim to a victory over the lowly human need for food, and, by extension, over all other lowly human dependencies—such as the need to give and receive love, to genuinely recognize and be recognized by others, to find joy in life.

At the end of the story, all avenues for the evasion of genuine self-awareness have been exhausted (most prominently by the hunger artist's inability to use the performance as a substitute for personal being). Kafka then creates, in the experience of reading, a palpable sense of a person, for the first time, entering tenderly, warily into genuine self-awareness. The experience of consciousnesses that is generated is at least as much an experience of self-awareness on the part of the author (as a felt presence in the language) as it is that of the character. The careful, loving manner in which the hunger artist-as-infant is held by the words of the narrator—"lips pursed, as if for a kiss" (Kafka, 1924, p. 277)—creates a sense of release from the cagelike mind/universe of a man who has been, until that moment, unseen and unseeing, unloved and unloving. It is not a release of a sort that involves the feeling of breaking through the bars of a cage; quite the opposite, it is a release in the form of a gentle lifting out"— "lifting his head a little" (Kafka, 1924, p. 277)—"an experience like that of picking up a baby from his crib to hold him in one's arms, in one's gaze, in one's love, and of being held in the infant's loving gaze.

This experience of consciousness, though a far richer experience than the one that occurred earlier in the story, is short-lived; this devolution bears the mark of Kafka's version of consciousness. Self-awareness—though achieved as a result of enormous effort—is inherently so painful that it can be sustained only momentarily. The pain of self-awareness in "A hunger artist" derives, at least in part, from the protagonist's recognition not only that he has never encountered the "food" (people or life experience) he liked, but also (by implication) that his inability to find that "food" may be a consequence of his inability to generate an appetite for engagement with other people or for life itself. And, at a still deeper level that he seems only barely to recognize, when he has experienced both appetite for, and joy in, the experience of loving and being loved, of recognizing and being recognized, he almost immediately, reflexively attempts to destroy it.

And yet, despite the hunger artist's flight from self-awareness, an extraordinary depth of self-redeeming consciousness is achieved and indelibly etched in the mind of the reader—and, I presume, in that of the author. The experience of achieving consciousness of something so fundamental to the truth of who one is, and of what one wants and needs, cannot be undone, taken back, or destroyed.

As discussed in Part I of this essay, Kafka creates the experience of the achievement of consciousness through the use of language, as opposed to the use of events that occur at the level of plot, or through explicit statement. Consciousness, for Kafka, is very much a literary event. The experience of writing fiction was a principal medium through which he achieved moments of human consciousness in a form that allowed him to attain genuine self-awareness of some of the truths of his existence without allowing those truths to destroy him.

The mark that Kafka left on the development of twentieth-century consciousness involves a sense that we spend our lives in an endless, largely futile search for ourselves; in the course of that search, we may achieve momentary glimpses (felt experiences) of who we are; but these glimpses, if they come at all, are limited in depth and short-lived. Nonetheless, these moments of self-awareness, though we reflexively flee from them, alter us profoundly and indelibly.

Consciousness was problematic for Borges in a way that was very different from the way in which it posed difficulties for Kafka. A fundamental difference, perhaps *the* fundamental difference, between what was entailed in Kafka's and Borges's efforts to achieve genuine consciousness inheres, I believe, in the fact that Borges's difficulties arose in an environment of love, while Kafka's were generated in an environment of fear, anger, and isolation. This difference can be felt in virtually every sentence of the two stories I have discussed.

For Borges, the universe as an infinite Library is a psychological/literary space in which the music and magic of words unfold endlessly, surprisingly, intelligently, humorously, darkly, ominously, and on and on. The universe for Kafka, in "A hunger artist," is a cage within which the protagonist spends almost the entirety of his life attempting to overcome his humanness by means of omnipotent, magical claims and beliefs. Consciousness is achieved momentarily through the intervention of a loving "overseer," but even this consciousness of love is rejected and defiled, though never entirely destroyed.

Consciousness is born at the intersection of the real and the imaginary. It is only when one can differentiate the two, and yet allow them to live in conversation with one another, that one may achieve self-awareness. The ground on which this intersection occurred for Borges was located, to a large degree, in the experience of reading and writing: the reality of the fulfilment of his promise to his father (to become the writer his father had aspired to be) was to be achieved by means of the exercise of literary skill and imagination. Borges, in his development as a writer and as a person, seemed to become increasingly aware not only of the infinite possibilities inherent in literary imagination, but also of the necessary limitations of words and ideas.

For Borges, the latter did not spoil the joy of the former. He found that imagination could not be allowed full rein or it would lose its tie to reality and become sheer fantasy, a literary genre lacking depth, complexity, and vitality. Borges believed that a fantastical story must contain only one fantastical element that unobtrusively finds its way, like a dream, into an otherwise ordinary reality; if there is more than one fantastical element, the story is mere science fiction. In this way, Borges was aware that fiction achieves its power only in relation to a reality that is a substantial, felt presence—as palpable as his experience of his father as a real and separate other person, and of their mutual love that was marked by its own distinctive quality of sadness.

In his nonliterary life, Borges had great difficulty in walking the ground on which reality and imagination meet, on which consciousness is born. Although he fell in love repeatedly, his love relationships were largely inventions of his own imagination, and consequently did not develop or endure (until very late in his life). He was unable to differentiate his fantasy of the "enlightened despot" from the reality of tyrants, such as Pinochet, for whom kidnapping, torture, and murder of tens of thousands of people were the basis of their power.

Kafka was able to negotiate the world that existed beyond his literary imagination somewhat better than Borges was able to do. Kafka was well aware of the circumstances in which reality trumps imagination—for example, in his understanding that he would have to train as a lawyer in order to earn a living, and that his mother was of little use to him in his effort to deal with his father.

Although Kafka and Borges differed in the ways they responded to many of the external realities of their lives, in the end, they were very much alike in relation to the ways in which they attempted to achieve consciousness of the truths of their lives. For both Borges and Kafka, writing was not an escape from reality or self-awareness. It was an entry into both. For Borges, the consciousness achieved in the act of writing such fictions as "The library of Babel" was characterized by a sense of discovering the wonders held by words and writing, including the power of words to endlessly expand meaning, to the point that words come to mean "everything and nothing" (Borges, 1960, p. 248). Achieving consciousness was, for Borges, predominantly a process of discovering/creating literary truths that were important to him in his experience of himself and others as readers and writers (for example, the ways in which authors create characters, who in turn create the author).

But consciousness, for Borges, also included the sad self-awareness that life in the Library (the universe of reading, writing, and the literary imagination) was a life made up only of books, that is, only of verbal renderings of other universes—for example, the universe of love and heartbreak lived out with real other people; the universe of the body and sexuality; the universe of experiences of real animal life, plant life, rivers, and mountains; and the infinite number of other universes making up life on earth.

For Kafka, consciousness achieved in the act of writing was a dangerous business in which he was forever walking on the very edge of an abyss. But walking at that edge while writing was what he lived for. Kafka approached and at times experienced a type of self-awareness that included the experience of loving and being loved, of seeing and being seen. His preoccupations were less exclusively literary than were those of Borges; he was as much concerned with the truths involved in becoming a man independent of his father and mother as he was in discovering/creating literary truths.

Borges, on the other hand, was truly a man of letters—a man who found and lost himself in "Borges," a literary creation who had a life in the real world. And it is there—in creating in his writing the experience of living in a borderland where the line between fiction and "real" life is blurred, where dreaming is part of waking life, where literary critics review imaginary books and where characters invent their authors—that Borges contributed most to the creation of human consciousness of his time, and of ours.

References

Barnstone, W. (1993). *With Borges on an ordinary evening in Buenos Aires: A memoir.* Urbana, IL/Chicago, IL: University of Illinois Press.

Borges, J. L. (1923). *Fervor de Buenos Aires.* In A. Coleman (ed.), *Jorge L. Borges: Selected poems* (pp. 1–32). New York: Viking, 1999.

Borges, J. L. (1932). A defense of the Kaballah. In E. Weinberger (ed.), *Jorge Luis Borges: Selected non-fictions* (pp. 83–86). (E. Allen, S. Levine, and E. Weinberger, Trans.). New York: Viking, 1999.

Borges, J. L. (1941a). The library of Babel. In D. Yates and J. Irby (eds), *Labyrinths: Selected stories and other writings* (pp. 51–58). (J. Irby, Trans.). New York: New Directions, 1964.

Borges, J. L. (1941b). The circular ruins. In D. Yates and J. Irby (eds), *Labyrinths: Selected stories and other writings* (pp. 45–50). (J. Irby, Trans.). New York: New Directions, 1964.

Borges, J. L. (1947). A new refutation of time. In D. Yates and J. Irby (eds), *Labyrinths: Selected stories and other writings* (pp. 217–234). (J. Irby, Trans.). New York: New Directions, 1964.

Borges, J. L. (1957). Borges and I. In D. Yates and J. Irby (eds), *Labyrinths: Selected stories and other writings* (pp. 246–247). (J. Irby, Trans.). New York: New Directions, 1964.

Borges, J. L. (1960). Everything and nothing. In D. Yates and J. Irby (eds), *Labyrinths: Selected stories and other writings* (pp. 248–249). (J. Irby, Trans.). New York: New Directions, 1964.

Borges, J. L. (1970). An autobiographical essay. In *The aleph and other stories, 1933–1969* (pp. 203–260). N. T. di Giovanni, in collaboration with J. L. Borges (ed. and Trans.). New York: Dutton.

Borges, J. L. (1984a). *Seven nights.* (E. Weinberger, Trans.). New York: New Directions.

Borges, J. L. (1984b). Conversation no. 6. In *Twenty-four conversations with Borges, including a selection of poems, interviews by Roberto Alifano, 1981–1983* (pp. 31–35). (N. Araúz, W. Barnstone, and N. Escandell, Trans.). Housatonic, MA: Lascaux Publishers.

Borges, J. L. (2000). *This craft of verse.* Cambridge, MA: Harvard University Press.

Burton, R. (1621). *The anatomy of melancholy*. (F. Dell and P. Jordan-Smith, eds). New York: Tudor Publishing, 1927.

Kafka, F. (1924). A hunger artist. In N. Glatzer (ed.), *Franz Kafka: The complete stories* (pp. 268–277). (W. Muir and E. Muir, Trans.). New York: Schocken Books, 1971.

Monegal, E. R. (1978). *Jorge Luis Borges: A literary biography*. New York: Paragon.

Williamson, E. (2004). *Borges: A life*. New York: Viking.

Woodall, J. (1996). *The man in the mirror of the book: A life of Jorge Luis Borges*. London: Hodder & Stoughton.

8

A CONVERSATION WITH
THOMAS H. OGDEN[1]

Luca Di Donna: What were the sources of inspiration in your early work that led you to embrace British Object Relations theory of unconscious process? Was it because of theoretical disagreement with the traditional American ego psychology or was it your own experiential work with patients that led you down this path?

Thomas H. Ogden: Luca, I became interested in psychoanalysis before I had a name for it. My mother was in analysis when I was a young child. She is a very sensitive and intelligent woman, so she didn't talk to me about psychoanalysis, but she did listen to me and speak to me from her experience in analysis. I only acquired a language for the sensibility that she brought to her mothering when, at 16, in high school, I was given a list of books from which to choose three for summer reading. Of the suggested books, I chose Freud's *A general introduction to psychoanalysis*. I can remember beginning to read it on a bus in New York City, and how I became so absorbed that I missed my stop, which didn't bother me at all since it meant that I could read undisturbed for as long as I chose. I was far more taken by the voice in the book than I was by the ideas. The book is written as an imaginary lecture to a skeptical audience. The way Freud speaks to the audience

---

1 I am indebted to San Francisco psychoanalyst Dr. Luca Di Donna for his lively and insightful contribution to this conversation.

about their doubts and fears concerning what he is saying was far more interesting to me then, and now, than the idea—for instance, the unconscious psychology of joke, or even the unconscious psychology of dreams. It was as if I already knew the content of the ideas—it felt to me that I had been familiar with the idea of the unconscious from the time I learned to talk, perhaps before.

In retrospect, I think that there were two reasons why the voice in the book was what interested me most—probably there were many reasons, but I'll mention only two. First, voice is a literary creation, and I loved Freud's writing as writing. I loved all good writing that my 16-year-old mind could be touched by.

The other reason I took to the voice in the book so thoroughly and readily was, I suppose, that it felt as if the voice I was hearing in the book was the voice of my mother's analyst, a voice I had been very curious about, and of course had never heard directly, but nonetheless was in my bones.

So my introduction to psychoanalysis was through object relations—my early relationship with my mother and, through her, my early relationship with her analyst and with psychoanalysis. This early experience with psychoanalysis was of a wordless sort, a sort that had to do with my very being and my mother's very being.

I haven't answered your question directly, but this is the most truthful way I can begin to tell the story. After I "discovered" psychoanalysis, or it discovered me, I read in a random sort of way the books that I happened to come upon. The second psychoanalytic book I read was Balint's *Primary love and psychoanalytic technique*, because it was the only book on psychoanalysis in the local library. I could feel the ways in which the voice and the writing style of this book differed greatly from Freud's. Balint was dealing with early forms of love, while Freud was concerned with early forms of sexuality. Even at my early age, I found love a more human event than the dissection of sexuality in which Freud was engaged.

I decided to go to medical school because, at the time, only medical doctors were admitted to psychoanalytic institutes associated with the American Psychoanalytic Association, which dominated American psychoanalysis. I didn't know that there were a very few institutes that admitted candidates who were not physicians. I'm not sure if I would not have taken the medical route even if I had been aware that I could become a psychoanalyst without doing so. I think that medical training does have value in the practice of psychoanalysis. For me, what was most important about my medical training was the experience of taking responsibility for the life of the patient in the most literal of ways. It is an enormous responsibility, and one that I think some analysts try to deny in their relationship with their patients. Most of the time, in psychoanalytic practice, patients are fully capable of taking responsibility for their own lives. But that is not always the case. For instance, schizophrenic patients and patients with other types of psychoses, along with depressed and suicidal patients, are often not able to take responsibility for their lives. Many analysts and psychotherapists whom I have treated or who have consulted with me are frightened of that type of responsibility and try to avoid it by not taking on psychotic or suicidal patients. Unfortunately for both the patient and the analyst, it is not always possible to predict which patients will become psychotic or suicidal in the course of the therapy or analysis. In fact, I believe that every analytic experience worth its salt involves psychotic and deeply depressed feeling states, and those states are avoided by analysts who are afraid of taking responsibility for the lives of their patients.

To bring this back to your question about American ego psychology and British Object Relations theory, I think that the latter analysts, for example, Winnicott, Fairbairn, Milner, Bion, Rosenfeld, and Segal, to name only a few, are far more willing to address the psychotic patient and the psychotic aspect of every patient than American ego psychologists are prepared to do. This was an important part of what drew me to British Object Relations theory. From the beginning of my residency training, I have been deeply interested in the treatment of seriously disturbed patients and have spent a good deal of my career as an analyst not only treating such patients, but also teaching and supervising therapists treating this group of patients.

LDD: You have written on a great variety of subjects. I've made a partial list of your wide-ranging interests, which, if you'll allow me to read this list in roughly chronological order, includes: the concept of projective identification; the psychoanalytic treatment of schizophrenia; the threshold of the male and female Oedipus complex; the initial analytic meeting; the Kleinian positions; Winnicott's potential space; the concept of internal object relations; the Freudian, Kleinian, and Winnicottian subjects; the analytic third; reverie; misrecognition; the autistic-contiguous position; analytic supervision; teaching psychoanalysis; psycho-analytic writing; as well as a series of papers in which you discuss the prose and poetry of Frost, Borges, Stevens, William Carlos Williams, and Kafka, plus another series of papers in which you write about your unique way of reading analytic writers, such as Freud, Isaacs, Fairbairn, Winnicott, Bion, Loewald, and Searles. I have failed to mention many other papers on still other subjects. When you look back on the almost forty years of writing in which you've been engaged, do you see a "project" or "line of development" in your work?

THO: Luca, I had hoped you would save your difficult questions for the end of the interview. Your question is one that I have asked myself many times. I think that there are a number of ideas that run through all of my work. The idea that it takes at least two people to think is the first one that comes to mind. I take up that idea in my early papers on projective identification. I rarely use the term any longer because everyone has their own definition of it, so I try to describe the phenomenon I'm talking about rather than use a term that has become stripped of meaning. What I have in mind when I talk about what I used to call "projective identification" is, in infancy, the mother and infant creating a third mind to which each contributes and from which each accrues individual meaning. Both give themselves over to the third, while at the same time retaining their individual identities, now changed by the experience of living in the third.

Genuine thinking is always on the move, "in flight," as William James put it. James, in 1900, concurrent with the publication of *The Interpretation of Dreams*, insisted that we should use verbs, adverbs, prepositions, and conjunctions, not nouns and adjectives, in describing all psychic events, since every psychic phenomenon is constantly changing. As James—the most undervalued psychol-ogist in the analytic literature—said, we ought to have words for feelings of *but*, and feelings of *and*, and feelings of *of*. I would put it in slightly different terms: We don't have memories, we remember sadly, dimly, hauntingly, and so on, and these ways of remembering transform us as we transform them, drown in them, and come back together in a form that is different from whom we had been, and is still in the process of changing. Change is the one constant in psychological states.

168

The conception of intersubjective thinking and feeling that I have been describing formed the basis of what I came to call "the analytic third," which is a concept that I must rediscover again and again if it is to hold any meaning for me. Sometimes, when I read other people's use of the term *analytic third*, I find the phenomenon that they are addressing new to me. The fact that I don't recognize my own thinking in another person's interpretation of the concept of the analytic third is an event that I welcome because it means that the interpretation of the concept has been nutriment for another person's thinking—that, after all, is the principal point of writing of any sort. The reader of a novel creates the characters, which is why it is almost always disappointing for me to see a film that is based on a novel I have loved—the characters in the film often kill my own images of the characters in the novel, and I'm left with someone else's images, which have little to do with my experience of reading and my very personal connection with the characters that the author and I have created.

Others, including the Barangers, Ferro, Civitarese, Chianese, and Bolognini, have used the metaphor of the analytic field to refer to two people thinking together—living in a world of co-constructed psychological and somatic forces that dictate particular ways of construing (giving meaning to) one's experience. The idea of a field and the idea of a third subject are simply metaphors for describing aspects of the analytic experience, the mother-infant relationship, and many other intimate emotional experiences. This is not to say that the two metaphors describe the same phenomena. No two metaphors describe the same thing—the whole point of using a metaphor is to create a unique way of describing one thing by comparing it to another. A force field is not a third subject—the ideas are related, but each views the experience of thinking together in different ways. For me, depending on the specific nature of the experience that the patient and I are having in the course of an analytic session, one metaphor or the other seems to better describe what is going on; very often, neither seems to work. I think in these conceptual terms after a session, or (for better and for worse) during a session when I am trying to find my footing outside of the experience I am having with the patient.

I find that the ideas that have developed in the course of my life as an analytic writer are inseparable from one another. For instance, a moment ago, in talking with you about the idea that it takes two or more people to think, I found myself talking about using verbs, adverbs, prepositions, conjunctions, and the nature of metaphors. My interest in language and my intrest in psycho-analysis have developed as inextricable parts of a whole.

LDD: To continue this discussion of the role of language in psychoanalysis, I would be interested to hear your thoughts on the importance of writing for you as an analyst. It is clear that writing has a specific meaning for you. Italian analysts have been interested in the conceptual ideas of writing in psychoanalysis for many years—such as in the work of Ferro, Racalbuto, and Semi. Your work has had a great impact on the Italian psychoanalytic community—not only for the clarity of your prose, but also for the affective involvement with the reader. Would you say something about what, for you, is the relationship between reading literature and the practice of analysis?

THO: Luca, literature has been a passion of mine throughout my life, and it seems to become all the more important as I get older. I view psychoanalysis and literature as holding in common a profound love and respect for language as a vehicle not simply for the *expression* of thoughts and feelings but, more important, as a medium for the *creation* of thoughts and feelings. We, in an important sense, are made of words. We transform our experience into thoughts and feelings in large part through the medium of language. As Bion and Ferro have demonstrated, each in their own way, visual imagery in dreaming, both while we are awake and asleep, carries out part of the transformation from raw experience to personal meaning. But I think that Freud's notion of the transformation of thing-presentations into word-presentations (in the transformation of unconscious experience into preconscious experience) is equally important to the creation of self-experience. I think that the role of language in human creation (as opposed to human expression) is valued by writers of literature and by psychoanalysts in ways that are very similar.

To take the idea that language makes us human a step further, I think that if we, as analysts, are to respond to what is uniquely human about each of our patients, we must develop with the patient an analytic conversation that we could have with no other person in the world. What I am saying is really quite familiar to all of us, whether we are in the mental health field or not: we speak to our spouse or partner in a way that we speak to no other person in the world. I am not referring to *what* we say, but to *the way we speak*. Similarly, we speak to our closest friend, our older daughter, our younger daughter, our brother, our father, our mother—to every person with whom we have an intimate relationship—in a way that we would not dream of speaking to anyone else in the world.

Parenthetically, the word *dream* that I used unintentionally has a great deal to do with the unique way we speak to the different people in our lives. The same is true of our conversations with our patients. I would hope that if one of my patients were somehow to hear me speaking to another of my patients, he or she would say, "I don't like the way you're talking. It's not that you're being seductive or parental or coercive, it just doesn't sound right to me." I would say, "That's what I hoped you would say. It wasn't meant for you, it's not something you and I created together. We didn't dream it up together." For me, creating a unique way of speaking with a patient is not a prerequisite for analytic work, it *is* the analytic work. When a patient can "speak his mind," he is creating himself—creating a self that he feels to be himself. When he has gone some distance in doing that, he will be able to talk to himself in his dreaming (in the medium of visual images) and in talking (in verbal and nonverbal ways) with others with whom he has intimate relationships. These conversations continue his analysis, that is, they continue to bring the patient into being through the media of imagistic language and verbal language.

The transference is a topic of conversation, which at times is very helpful in understanding something of what it is that is preventing the patient from "speaking his mind." I don't find that the term *interpretation* well describes how I speak to patients. I think the phrase "talking with the patient" better captures the feeling of the conversations I have with patients than does the phrase "making an interpretation." I take it as high praise when a patient asks me, "Why don't you ever make interpretations?" This, to me, does not mean I'm not thinking psychoanalytically; it means I'm not talking psychoanalytically. To talk psycho-analytically is to speak in a foreign tongue, a tongue I haven't created. I try to speak in my own tongue, though this is a very difficult thing to do.

The idea of uniqueness of voice brings me back to the influence that reading poetry and fiction has on my thinking and working as an analyst. To learn what it means to speak in one's

171

own tongue, there is no better place to go than to the great writers. No one in the history of the world wrote the way Borges wrote. If someone were to do so, he would be simply an imitator of Borges. The same is true of Kafka, Calvino, Homer, Coetzee, Wordsworth, Melville, Beckett, and Frost—to name only a handful of my favorite writers. To these and other great writers is where I go not only to witness, but to take part in, the creation of a tongue of my own.

LDD: Tom, your love for language and literature is thought provoking. Reading your latest book, *Creative readings*, I loved your commentaries on selected texts of Freud, Isaacs, Fairbairn, Winnicott, Bion, Loewald, and Searles. I'm thinking here of love as a way of discovering something new—in this case, discovering something new in these texts. Your reading is persuasive, which opens new ways of understanding—illuminating the dark spot of these important thinkers. It seems that the authors whom you chose were psychoanalysts who were not afraid to go beyond established canon. They were nonconformist, a bit visionary, independent thinkers who also maintained a love for their ancestors. Could you say more about your passion for these authors and how you make use of them as your psychoanalytic ancestors?

THO: When you use the phrase *psychoanalytic ancestors*, the first thought that comes to mind is Borges's essay in which he says that Kafka created his own ancestors. I think that I, and all other readers, create our own ancestors in that we find—or perhaps create— ourselves in the writing of our forebears. We find an unrealized potential in their work from which we discover not only who they were, but who we are. For the past decade, in the series of articles collected in *Leggere creativamente* [*Creative readings*], I have, without ever putting it in this way to myself, created my own psycho- analytic family tree. In writing about the work of these authors, I have in a sense rewritten their work in a way that is my own, and in another sense, they have rewritten me by means of their influence on me. I have used their works in much the same way that Winnicott describes the infant's use of the mother as a mirror. Let me explain what I mean by this comparison. Winni- cott's ideas about the mirror function of the mother are regularly misstated in a way that not only misleads, but turns something essential to development into something pathological. So often I read and hear analysts describe Winnicott's ideas of the mirror- role of the mother as "the infant seeing himself in the eyes of the

172

mother." What Winnicott actually says is that the infant sees "something *like* himself" in the eyes of the mother. The latter is a symbolic function in which the infant sees himself *transformed* in the eyes of the mother—he sees the mother's interpretation of him, or to use other words, the infant sees the metaphor that his mother has created to express the impression that her infant has made on her. The transformation of himself that the infant sees in the eyes of his mother exists in a non-verbal symbolic sphere. The infant that the infant sees in his mother's eyes is not his mirror image (his double). Rather, what he sees is *his* impression, the mark *he has made* on another person, an impression with which the mother has done something of her own.

From this perspective, the infant's experience of seeing something *like* himself in his mother's eyes is an experience of connection with someone who is *not* he. In that way, the mirror experience is an experience of separation in two different senses. First, it is an experience of separateness from the mother, who is a separate person who makes metaphors of her own with her experience of the infant. At least as important, the infant's experience of seeing a metaphorical transformed version of himself in the eyes of another is a critical event in the infant's development of his own capacity for consciousness, self-awareness. In the infant's experience of seeing the metaphor that the mother has created for *her experience of him*, two versions of the infant become real in the infant's mind simultaneously: the infant-as-perceiving-self (I) and the infant-as-object of the mother's perception (me). The space between the observing infant (I) and the observed infant seen in the mother's eyes (me) is the space in which the experience of consciousness is born, the space in which the infant is simultaneously the observing self and the observed self.

I find in the experience of reading the work of great analytic thinkers something of the mirror-role experience I have just discussed. I see their ideas as metaphors for my own thinking (thinking I am doing in the process of reading their work). I cannot emphasize enough that it is in *their* ideas, ideas that are *not* my creations, that I find reflections (transformations) of myself that I had not previously known. It is that transformation of myself that I use to rewrite their work in a way that is original—that is, what I write is my own thinking, which is at once separable from theirs (they are my own original ideas) and inseparable from theirs (my ideas are transformations of theirs). To put it in still other terms, they have seen me in a way that I have not yet seen myself; and I read them in a way that they have not yet been seen. It is in this sense that I create my own ancestors who create me as I read their work.

To conceive of ancestry in this way is to reject the notion of strictly chronological time. The movement of influence (and time) is not only from past to present to future. Movement of influence and time is also from future to present to past. We who are the present readers of Freud, Isaacs, and Winnicott alter the past (transform their work as they understood it) in our present act of transforming (reinventing) what they wrote. Most important, in making their work our own, we are coming into being as thinkers in our own right, whose ideas others in the future will make use of in the process of creating themselves in ways that are unimaginable to us now.

LDD: In the course of the decades that you've been practicing psychoanalysis, what seems to you to lie at its core?

THO: Two things immediately come to mind in response to your question. The first is the importance of being humane. Without that as a defining characteristic of the analyst, there is nothing that is psychoanalytic about the experience occurring between analyst and patient. I've had many people, both candidates and people outside the mental health profession, consult me with regard to difficulties in their personal analyses. Almost always, the analyst has not been able to handle the countertransference and has become inhumane in his or her way of being with the patient. Sometimes this takes the form of the analyst's treating the patient as if she were an enemy to his well-being, his integrity, his reputation, and so on. And in almost every case, it has seemed to me that, unconsciously, the analyst has experienced what is going on between him and the patient as a threat to his sanity. In response to this threat, the analyst counterattacks by conducting himself in a way that he believes will threaten the sanity of the patient. As a consequence of his knowing the patient at the depth that he does, he is in a position to do a very good job of locating what is most terrifying to the patient.

While I cannot go into detail for reasons of confidentiality, the analyst's counterattack has in some cases taken the form of exploiting the patient's transference feelings of utter dependence. In these instances, the analyst has explicitly or implicitly threatened to cut his ties with the patient in such a way that conveys the feeling that no other analyst or therapist will have anything to do with such a repellent and dangerous patient. Not only is the analyst going to abandon the patient, he conveys to the patient the idea that everyone else in the world will also leave the patient, and so the patient will find herself alone in the world, unable to take care of herself, and ultimately will die or lose her mind, which amount to the same thing. This is what I mean by inhumane treatment of a patient. This is no longer psychoanalysis.

The other thing that came to mind concerning your question regarding what I view as most central to psychoanalysis is something that is so old as to be a cliché, and yet I believe it is often a neglected or dismissed idea. What I have in mind is the idea that psychoanalysis is not only a "talking therapy," it is a "conversation therapy." It is not enough for the analyst to listen to the patient with "evenly hovering attention," as Freud put it, and to make well-timed interpretations of the transference. Even if this were to be done with the greatest skill and accuracy, I believe, on the basis of supervising analysts who work this way, that the patient becomes better able to observe himself and make connections between past and present experience. But self-knowledge is not sufficient to effect fundamental psychological growth. The analytic experience, to my mind, is the experience of talking *with* another person, not an experience of talking *to* another person. The latter often seems to me to constitute something comparable to children's parallel play. The former, a *conversation* in which two people are talking with one another, involves a different sort of structuring of language and structuring of experience. The spoken conversation resonates with an unconscious conversation in which the two people are thinking together. Thinking together is the other essential feature of psychoanalysis that I have in mind. As I said earlier, it takes two people to think—that is, it requires the creation of a form of unconscious thinking made up of the conjoint thinking and feeling of two people, which enables them to think in a way that neither individual alone could think/feel. It is that experience of thinking with another person with whom one is in conversation, consciously and unconsciously, that I believe has the potential to create conditions in which psychological change may occur in both the patient and the analyst.

There is much else that constitutes the core of psychoanalysis, but these are aspects of an analytic experience that seem essential to me.

LDD: Tom, you have introduced the concept of the "analytic third." How does that concept differ from the concept of the "analytic field"?

THO: I find myself using both terms. Which of the two I use depends on which aspect of an analytic experience I am trying to think or speak about. Both concepts are metaphors, and each emphasizes a different aspect of mental functioning. The mind is not a material thing—you can't see it, measure it, or even locate it. It doesn't occupy a space between our ears. Despite the fact that I know that, I can't stop myself from imagining that the mind is "in" our heads. But since that is a misconception and the mind is not a material thing, we use metaphors to think about mental functioning that are drawn from the physical world. The concept of an analytic field borrows from physics in that it is comparing the interplay of invisible psychic forces with the interplay of forces in such fields as electromagnetic fields and gravitational force fields. The metaphor of an analytic field places emphasis on the ways in which force fields are generated by the interaction of differing "poles" and on the way in which forces of enormous strength can be generated by events that are invisible.

The concept of the analytic third is a metaphor that is analogous to "emergence theory," a set of ideas currently being developed by theorists in the natural sciences. Emergence theory holds that matter and energy of one category hold the potential to combine in ways that yield a product that is entirely different in nature from the combining elements, and consequently wholly unpredictable. The most dramatic example of "emergence" of this sort is the creation of life from the combination of inanimate chemicals and electrical forces. The metaphor of the "analytic third" places less emphasis on the force field created by the conscious and unconscious experience of two people than it does on the creation of a third mind, a third subjectivity, that is irreducible to the sum of the two subjectivities that go into its formation. The analytic third is a metaphor for the creation of a mind that has an existence of its own and is capable of thinking in ways that neither contributor to the creation of the third subject is capable of generating on his own. As you can hear as I describe the metaphor of the analytic third, there is a danger of using the metaphor too concretely. For instance, when thinking concretely, one might ask, "Is this a third person who has no body?" and "Can a third mind without a body have bodily experiences?"

Of course, taking the metaphor as a physical fact produces these and other absurdities. Every metaphor reaches its breaking point when stretched too far or used too concretely. The important thing is that when we use metaphors, we remember that they are only metaphors, and that we have to use other metaphors or invent new ones when the old ones reach their breaking point or become stale.

Of course, the metaphor of the analytic field has its limits, too. If it is taken literally and not metaphorically, absurd questions arise, such as: What is a mental force field? Does the unconscious of each of the two people "come into contact" with that of the other? What does "contact" mean in a mental field?

LDD: Under what circumstances do you find yourself using one metaphor or the other—the analytic field or the analytic third?

THO: That's a difficult question. Let me think a little about that because I shift between the two in a way that feels natural, but I don't have strict boundary lines between the two.

The two concepts predominantly overlap. This is just an impression, but I think I tend to use the concept of the analytic field when I'm thinking about an analytic situation that involves the frame and the sorts of pressures that are being unconsciously exerted on the analyst in relation to the frame.

I think I tend to use the concept of the analytic third when thinking about reverie and the ways in which it is the expression of thoughts and feelings that are not the exclusive creation of either the analyst or the analysand. I think of the patient's dreams in a similar way—they are not to be taken exclusively as the patient's creation. But I would not want these first impressions to be taken as a statement of the "correct" context in which these two metaphors are to be applied. Each person will use the metaphors of the analytic third and the analytic field in ways that work best in their efforts to think about what is occurring at any given moment in an analytic experience. And before too long, both metaphors will become stale and others will have to be invented.

LDD: You and your son Benjamin have written a book together on psychoanalysis and literary criticism—*The analyst's ear and the critic's eye: Rethinking psychoanalysis and literary criticism*. I understand that it has been published in English as well as Italian in the spring. Would you tell me a little about your experience of writing that book with your son?

177

THO: Writing that book with Ben was one of the most fulfilling and enjoyable experiences of my life. It is an extraordinary thing to work on a project of that sort with one's child who is no longer a child, but an accomplished literary scholar. People ask me if there was a great deal of competition and hostility in our writing a book together. Each time, I'm surprised by the question because there was no hostility on either of our parts. Co-authoring the book was a wonderful medium for our getting to know one another as adults.

Part of what made the experience so enjoyable was being able to learn so much from Ben. I was quite surprised by Ben's ability to make very insightful observations about assumptions I've consistently made without being aware of them in the literary criticism I've written. For instance, he pointed out that I tend to privilege voice over other aspects of the author's use of language, without justifying why I believe that voice, in a particular passage, is a more important aspect of the use of language in that passage than syntax, for instance, or the literary genre being alluded to. He also pointed out that I assume that if a poem or novel evokes a particular feeling state, the author must have at one time or another—perhaps only in writing the piece—experienced that set of feelings. When he made that observation, I said, "The characters are fictions, so they can't feel anything. Who else but the author could be feeling the feelings evoked by the story?" He asked, "Why isn't it possible that an author is sufficiently skilled in his use of language to compellingly create any feeling state in a text?" I said that I didn't think that an author could convincingly write in a way that evoked a set of feelings he had never experienced.

Ben said that that was a belief on my part, and he wasn't going to try to talk me out of it, but it was an assumption that I should be aware of. He added that he has the same doubts about that idea as I do, but it's interesting to hold the question in the back of your mind as you read or as you write literary criticism.

LDD: How did you structure the book in terms of your two perspectives? Did you enter into conversation?

THO: No, we decided not to structure the book as a conversation between a psychoanalyst and a literary critic. We use the narrative "we" to speak to the reader. The "we" changes in the course of the book as the two of us learn from one another and become capable of a more complex understanding of the relationship between psychoanalysis and literary criticism.

LDD: I look forward to reading the book. In your last two books, *This art of psychoanalysis* and *Rediscovering psychoanalysis*, I've noticed a change in your theoretical position. It seems that you are moving away from a language that is explanatory to a more affective language in order to reach the patient.

THO: That's a very perceptive observation. I wouldn't have thought to put it that way, but I think that it is true. As I said earlier, I increasingly think of the analytic dialogue as a conversation of a sort that occurs under no other circumstances. I do not see the structure of the dialogue between patient and analyst as one in which the analyst listens, and then, after he gathers his thoughts and comes to an understanding of the unconscious meanings of the patient's communications, offers an interpretation. Rather, I see the analytic pair as dreaming together. Each has the opportunity to say what he or she believes to be true and utilizable by the other, within the terms of their relationship of doctor and patient. This latter part is essential: the analyst, while being an equal of the patient, has a decidedly different role and responsibility from that of the patient. I'll get back to that in a minute. For the moment, let me continue with a response to your question. I don't see my role as that of giving the patient a guided tour of his or her unconscious mind. There is nothing mutative or growth promoting about the acquisition of greater knowledge *about* oneself. What is mutative, I believe, is the experience *of* oneself in the context of *being with* another person who recognizes you to be the person you are and the person you are in the process of becoming. The analytic experience of *being with* another person is unique in that the analytic relationship, with its odd setting of the patient on the couch and the analyst out of sight behind the patient, promotes a relationship in which dreaming together is a principal medium of unconscious communication and a principal source of thoughts and feelings *about which* the patient and analyst talk with one another and *from which* the analyst speaks to the patient.

As I speak about these ideas as generalities about the way I currently work with patients, I hope not to give the impression that there is a sameness about the experience that I have with my patients. I said this earlier, but I cannot emphasize strongly enough that the experience I have in analysis with each patient is unique to that patient. It is essential that the patient and I dream up an analytic experience that is unique to that patient and me.

It is also essential that I rediscover psychoanalysis with each patient. With one patient I'm thinking of, discussion of our relationship, that is, the transference, was critical to psychological growth (on the patient's part and my own).

With another patient, I chose not to discuss our relationship for many years, even though I was giving it a great deal of thought in every session. I would not say that the transference was more important in the analysis of the first patient than in the analysis of the second. Rather, I would say that explicit discussion of the transference was more important to the first analysis than it was to the second in those years of the analyses.

Let me return to the thought I put to the side a few minutes ago, which had to do with the analyst's responsibility as doctor to the patient. I recoil when I hear analysts speak or write about their responsibility to psychoanalysis and the necessity of holding to that responsibility because it is the best thing that we have to offer patients. I also recoil from the idea that the analyst should not be concerned with the outcome of the analysis, since change is up to the patient and out of the hands of the analyst. I believe quite the contrary to these attitudes. I feel strongly that my responsibility is not to psychoanalysis, but to the patient. My responsibility is to offer the patient the best treatment I can for his particular psychological and physical problems. To put it more strongly, my sole responsibility is to the patient and to others in his life if they are being treated inhumanely by him. I am the patient's doctor in the broad sense of the word *doctor*, not the strictly medical sense that we discussed earlier. If the patient is able to use psychoanalysis, I attempt to invent a form of it that is optimal for him. If the patient is suffering from an illness, such as alcohol or drug addiction, I refer him to a treatment program that offers help to such patients—psychoanalysis has a notoriously poor track record in the treatment of drug-addicted patients.

As I'm saying this, an analyst who consults with me on his clinical work comes to mind. He recently had a patient collapse in his consulting room. The patient had had similar episodes in the recent past, but had done nothing about them. The analyst, who had been a doctor of internal medicine early in his career, decided to drive the patient to the patient's sister's house nearby. She then took the patient to the hospital, where a thorough medical work-up was conducted. I believe that that was the most therapeutic thing for that analyst to do for that patient. It is not a prescription for any other analytic pair. That situation could not occur between any other patient and analyst. What I take from that example is the analyst's freedom to attempt to be the doctor that the patient needed under the circumstances. I believe that being the best doctor one can be for one's patient is also to be the best analyst one can be to that patient. An analyst is not a person who practices psychoanalysis an analyst is a person who brings an analytic sensibility, training, and experience to his work with his patients.

LDD: Tom, how do you think about the question of trauma in general, and generationally transmitted trauma in particular. The latter is ubiquitous but has deep roots in South Africa, the Balkans, the American South, Northern Ireland, and in the areas rocked by the Holocaust.

THO: Luca, I think of trauma as unthinkable experience. Trauma is an event that is too much—too disturbing, too unbearable for an individual to think and feel. No genuine dreaming, that is, unconscious psychological work, can be done with the experience. The upshot of these experiences that cannot be dreamt, these "undreamt dreams," include physical illness, repetitive and unchanging nightmares, night terrors, and autistic withdrawal.

Traumata require at least two people to think and feel the event. I think that some traumas can only be processed in a group setting. As an individual, one inevitably reaches the limits of what one's own personality system is able to think/dream, and it is at that point, that limit, that one develops symptoms that mark the place where one's thoughts are unthinkable/undreamable and can go no further. If one is fortunate enough not to be alone with traumatic experiences (which are always alive in the present), one may get help from one or more other people in thinking/dreaming one's previously unthinkable experience. A person so fortunate as not to be alone with his or her trauma engages another person or people in helping him/her think/feel what cannot be experienced alone. That other person or people may be a spouse, a friend, a sibling, or an analyst. In conversation with another person or people, the two (or more) bring to bear something larger than a single personality system. What is brought to bear on the unthinkable thought is also larger than the sum of the individual personality systems. The two or more people create an unconscious third subject that is capable of thinking what none of the people alone is capable of thinking, and taking in, in a transformative way.

Often, two people, or ten people, are not sufficient to think the unthinkable thought because all of those involved in the attempt at thinking have suffered from similar traumas. That group of people may constitute an entire generation of people—for instance, a generation (or two or three) of South Africans (both blacks and whites) who lived the experience of apartheid, or generations of Northern Irish people (both Catholics and Protestants) during "the troubles." The enormity of understatement in the term "the troubles" is, I believe, a reflection of the degree to which the murders, massacres, and terrorizing cannot be thought, much less spoken.

Sometimes a person from within the traumatized generations—for example, Nelson Mandela or Desmond Tutu—may be able to help an entire nation of people to think the formerly unthinkable. The same can be said of Gandhi. I think Martin Luther King performed this function in relation to the generational trauma of slavery in the United States. I have no illusion that two or three individuals can transform a nation's unthinkable into the thinkable, dreamable, and speakable, but I do believe that they can make a difference.

LDD: I would like to thank you for your time and consideration.

THO: It has been a great pleasure talking with you about these topics that are so important for both of us.

Index

illusion: magical thinking 21; mother able to create 58

improvisation: as analysis 108

indwelling 53

internalization 98

internal object relations 33–4; 167

internal saboteur 64

interpretation: "all the work has been done" 81; and analytic conversation 171; evolution of 85–7, 88; pre-packaged 64; talking about psychic reality 86–7; 88–9; of transference 37n, 62, 64, 107, 175; and the unknown 81; when "not really an analyst" 93

The interpretation of dreams 168

intersubjective: analytic third 28, 85, 101, 168–9, 176–7; development of analyst 94–5; mother–infant 28–9; process in analysis 28–9; reverie 79; thinking 34, 94, 168–9;

intuition: and at-one-ment 80; and psychic reality 72, 77–80, 89; and truth 6; unbidden 80; and unknown 80–1

Ionesco, E. 96

Irby, J. 125n1

Isaacs, S. 168, 172, 174

Italian psychoanalytic community 170

James, H. 96

James, W. 168

Jesenska, M. 123, 124

Jung, C. G. 105

Jungian archetypal unconscious 56

"K" 27; movement from to "O" 33

Kaballah 155

Kafka, F.: alters structure of thinking 115; *Amerika* 123; anti-Semitism 118; Bauer, F. 120–22; biographical sketch 116–124;

Brod, M. 117, 118–22, 123–4, 135; *The castle* 123; Daimont, D. 123, 124; death camps 124; *Diaries 1910–1923* 117, 118–22; failure 116–7, 134; father 117, 118; "A hunger artist" 124, 125–135, 158–60; hypochondria 120; independence 120; Jesenska, M. 123, 124; *Kafkaesque* 115; Klopstock, R. 124; *Letter to his father* 117, 122; lonely childhood 117–8; "Metamorphosis" 119; mother 117; The Prague Four 118; recognition 123; relationship to his art 139; sister Ottla 122–3; somatic difficulties 120; "The stoker" 119; struggle with human consciousness 116, 134–5, 158–61, 162; translated by Borges 140, 144, 145; *The trial* 119, 122, 123; tuberculosis 122–3; Worker's Accident Insurance Institute 119

Kafka, O. 123

Kieslowski, K. 96

King, M. L. 182

Klein, M.: control, contempt, and triumph 20; depressive position 18, 33, 167; *Melanie Klein today: Volume 2 Mainly practice* 72; "Notes on some schizoid mechanisms" 47; paranoid schizoid position 18, 33, 167; symbolic meaning in children's play 86; as teacher 3; transformation for psychological growth 33

Klopstock, R. 124

Kodama, M. 148, 149

Kohan-Miller, Dr. 146

Kubrick, S. 54

Lange, N. 143

Langs, R. 72

language: action of 125; Bion's 73, 76; blunt 9; Borges's 140, 141,